John Dygon's *Proportiones practicabiles secundum Gaffurium*
(Practical proportions according to Gaffurius)

Containing two separate but very closely related texts on arithmetic proportions and their application in the rhythmic notation of polyphonic music, this slender and enigmatic manuscript of unmistakable English origin written in the first half of the sixteenth century (Cambridge, Trinity College, O.3.38) is now edited and translated for the first time. The redactor was the monk John Dygon, prior of St. Augustine's Monastery in Canterbury at the Dissolution and the holder of a bachelor's degree in music from the University of Oxford; but the treatises of the Cambridge manuscript, rather than presenting a new and independent treatment of proportions in polyphony, are in fact largely extracted and paraphrased from Book IV of the *Practica musice* of Franchinus Gaffurius, first printed in Milan in 1496. Replacing the musical examples of the celebrated Italian treatise with newly composed works, Dygon adapted Gaffurius's text to increase its relevance for English practitioners. As an item within the traditions of English theoretical writing at the end of the Middle Ages, the treatise represents a unique example of direct derivation from a single near-contemporaneous continental treatise, and as a source (though peripheral) for one of the major theoretical works of the period, the English book is significant on account of the amount of material that has been modified and adapted.

Theodor Dumitrescu is a STUDIUM postdoctoral research fellow at the Centre d'Études Supérieures de la Renaissance (Tours).

Studies in the History of Music Theory and Literature

Thomas J. Mathiesen,
General Editor

volume 2

Theodor Dumitrescu

John Dygon's *Proportiones practicabiles secundum Gaffurium*
(Practical proportions according to Gaffurius)

New Critical Text, Translation, Annotations, and Indices

University of Illinois Press
Urbana and Chicago

Manufactured in the United States of America
C 5 4 3 2 1
∞ This book is printed on acid-free paper.

Complete Cataloging-in-Publication information
is on file at the Library of Congress.

ISBN-10 0-252-03182-2
ISBN-13 978-0-252-03182-3

LATINITATIS CUSTODI REGINALDO FOSTER

CONTENTS

Series Editor's Preface

We are pleased to present in this volume John Dygon's *Proportiones practicabiles secundum Gaffurium*, a remarkable adaptation of part of Franchino Gaffurio's *Practica musice* for English practitioners. Theodor Dumitrescu has prepared the first critical edition and translation of the treatise and introduced it with a masterful illumination of the author's life, the English theoretical tradition, and the design and content of the treatises. As this volume also represents the first of a new series of critical texts and translations intended to continue and expand the tradition of my former series *Greek and Latin Music Theory*, it seems appropriate to review the principles of that earlier series and assure readers that the tradition has found a congenial new home.

Studies in the History of Music Theory and Literature has as its goal the publication of specialized monographs dealing with the history of music theory and music literature, such as the first volume in the series, Claude V. Palisca's *Music and Ideas in the Sixteenth and Seventeenth Centuries* (or, in more general terms, writings about music or connected to music that are not technically music theory, such as music historiography, musical aesthetics, the history of criticism, rhythmics and metrics, the development of operatic librettos, etc.); collective volumes (e.g., *Music in the Mirror*, which grew out of a conference of the same name); reference tools pertaining to the history of music theory (e.g., *Thesaurus Musicarum Latinarum: Canon of Data Files*, a composite index of all the electronic texts contained in the *Thesaurus Musicarum Latinarum*); annotated translations of music theory without a facing-page original text in cases where the original text may already be readily available; and—especially—critical texts and translations in parallel format with extended introductions and annotations, including works in all languages, not only in Greek and Latin.

Naturally, the editorial principles will vary according to the type of publication, but for critical texts and translations, *Studies in the History of Music Theory and Literature* will continue the tradition of presenting the original text on facing pages with the translation, fully annotated to illuminate the content of the treatise. As in the present volume, each volume will include a major introductory essay discussing, as appropriate, the significance of the treatise to its theoretical tradition; the life of its author (or, for anonymous works, the probable authors); the design, sources, and theoretical premises of the treatise; the manuscripts or other sources used to establish the text; *loci paralleli* and quotations; and special considerations involved in the translation. The texts will be based on a full collation of every relevant source—insofar as possible—and the collation will be represented in a critical apparatus at the bottom of each text page. The translations are intended to be readable, but at the same time, they will attempt to preserve in large measure the consistency, variety, tone, and style of the original, Special care will be given to the treatment of technical vocabulary, syntactic subtleties, and consistency of terminology. Finally, each volume will include indices of words, names, and subjects.

A number of additional critical texts and translations are already underway as future volumes for *Studies in the History of Music Theory and Literature*, and we anticipate the publication of one or two volumes a year. Proposals for future volumes are, of course, always welcome, as are your inquiries, suggestions, or other comments about the series.

Thomas J. Mathiesen
General Editor,
Studies in the History of Music Theory and Literature

Center for the History of
Music Theory and Literature
Eigenmann Hall 702
Jacobs School of Music
Indiana University
Bloomington, IN 47405

Preface and Acknowledgments

An initial study and edition of the Cambridge treatises formed part of my doctoral thesis at the University of Oxford (2004). The greatly expanded and revised version in the present volume was completed during the tenure of a fellowship at the Centre d'Études Supérieures de la Renaissance (Tours) with the financial support of le STUDIUM.

For comments, criticisms, and suggestions for improvement I am especially grateful to Margaret Bent, Bonnie Blackburn, Thomas Mathiesen, Ronald Woodley, and the anonymous external reviewers of this text for the University of Illinois Press. I would like to thank the staff of the Wren Library and the Master and Fellows of Trinity College, Cambridge, for access to the manuscript and permission to reproduce several of its pages.

INTRODUCTION

The Cambridge Treatises and the English Traditions

The survival into modern times of English music theory from the early Tudor period is remarkably sparse. For investigators tracing the conceptual systems underlying insular polyphonic composition in the early sixteenth century, it is telling that the evidence from literary remains has been treated as one of our major sources of specific technical information and terminology.[1] Surviving documents dedicated primarily to music theory are limited to three manuscripts, one of which consists for the most part of direct copies from one of the others and has little independent value.[2] As a result, the study of English theory from this period is an endeavor requiring a considerable measure of imaginative reconstruction, based on materials from surrounding periods whose teachings enjoyed some amount of continuity throughout the fifteenth and sixteenth centuries. To date, only a portion of the early-Tudor theoretical material is available in published editions or translations.[3]

The present volume offers for the first time a transcription and translation of the enigmatic manuscript O.3.38 of Trinity College, Cambridge (**GB**-Ctc), a theory book of unmistakable English origin written in the first half of the sixteenth century. Containing two separate but very closely related texts on arithmetic proportions and their application in the rhythmic notation of polyphonic music, this slender manuscript thus presents information that has a direct bearing on practical counterpoint (i.e., composition and improvi-

[1] Cf. Roger Bray, "Music and Musicians in Tudor England: Sources, Composition Theory and Performance," in *The Blackwell History of Music in Britain: The Sixteenth Century*, ed. Roger Bray (Oxford: Blackwell, 1995), 3–6.

[2] Cambridge, Trinity College (**GB**-Ctc), O.3.38; London, British Library (**GB**-Lbl), Additional 10336; and London, Lambeth Palace (**GB**-Llp), 466. The contents of these books are discussed further below. Library sigla throughout accord with those assigned by the *Répertoire International des Sources Musicales*; for a complete listing of the sigla, see the *Conspectus codicis et notarum* (p. 67 *infra*).

[3] Ronald Woodley, *John Tucke: A Case Study in Early Tudor Music Theory* (Oxford: Clarendon Press; New York: Oxford University Press, 1993). Woodley's investigation includes transcriptions and translations of extracts from **GB**-Lbl Add. 10336, most of which were recopied into **GB**-Llp 466 as well.

sation). The redactor of at least the first text in the book was the monk John Dygon, prior of St. Augustine's Monastery in Canterbury at the Dissolution and probably the holder of a bachelor's degree in music from the University of Oxford;[4] the close textual and musical relations between the two sections of the book, moreover, point to Dygon as the author of the entire contents of the manuscript. The ascription to Dygon, however, must receive a significant qualification: the treatises of the Cambridge manuscript, rather than presenting a new and independent treatment of proportions in polyphony, are in fact largely extracted and paraphrased from Book IV of the *Practica musice* of Franchinus Gaffurius, first printed in Milan in 1496.[5] Replacing the musical examples of the celebrated Italian treatise with newly composed works, Dygon further adapted Gaffurius's text to increase its relevance for English practitioners. As an item within the traditions of English theoretical writing at the end of the Middle Ages, the writing in **GB**-Ctc O.3.38 represents a unique case in being derived directly from a single near-contemporaneous continental treatise; and as a source (though peripheral) for one of the major theoretical works of the period, the English book is no less peculiar, on account of the amount of material that has been modified and adapted.

The application of proportional theory in the rhythmic context of mensural notation, of course, was by no means a new development for English writing of the sixteenth century. The purely mathematical aspects of the proportion system formed a core component of classical *musica speculativa* or *musica theorica* in the derivation of musical intervals and the division of the monochord. In this form, proportion theory would have been a regular element in university teaching and was well represented in writings concerned solely with arithmetic. Students traditionally encountered the musical aspects of these teachings primarily through the required study of Boethius's *De institutione musica*, for many centuries the basic music textbook at universities throughout Europe. The extension of the system in a direct way into the sphere of *musica practica*, however, was a phenomenon

---

[4]See "The Author of the Treatises" *infra*. This John Dygon is not to be confused with two other men of the same name: one, the abbot of St. Augustine's monastery from 1497 to 1509; the other, a priest working in the first half of the fifteenth century who was active in creating and donating manuscripts to Magdalen College, Oxford (see Ralph Hanna, "Producing Magdalen College MS lat. 93," *Yearbook of English Studies* 33 [2003]: 142–55).

[5]Franchinus Gaffurius, *Practica musice* (Milan: Ioannes Petrus de Lomatio, 1496; reprint, New York: Broude Bros., 1979); see Rufus Hallmark, "An Unknown English Treatise of the 16th Century," *Journal of the American Musicological Society* 22 (1969): 273–74.

that accompanied the new rhythmic developments of the fourteenth century.[6]

As the flexible and varied notational innovations of the *ars nova* solidified into a more unified mensural notation system, a number of notational configurations gave rise to the possibility of rhythmic proportionality: an unequal basic relationship between the lengths of the same type of note in different contexts, sounding simultaneously or successively. It is generally agreed that rhythmic proportions gained compositional favor on account of the possibility of simultaneously using minimae of different lengths in different voices, bypassing the default minima equivalence of the French rhythmic system.[7] The concept probably did not spring from a single source: the fourteenth-century Italian system of notation offers some scope for basic proportionality, and Johannes de Muris himself mentions the division of the brevis into differing numbers of semibreves. It is nevertheless certain and germane to the present discussion that the impetus for the new rhythmic possibilities arose from practical experimentation with the mensural notation system, which in its earliest forms utilized mainly those configurations that related to the comparative treatment of different basic mensurations. By the end of the fourteenth century and in the early fifteenth century, advanced composers could use a number of notational devices to indicate proportions, including Hindu-Arabic numerals, coloration, and the simple combination (or succession) of different mensurations without minima equivalence. The theoretical tradition of describing the rhythmic treatment of proportions appears to have arisen at much the same time: the earliest securely datable specimen is the *Tractatus practice de musica mensurabili* (1408) of Prosdocimus de Beldemandis.[8]

---

[6]The distinction in usage is recognized, for example, in the practical discussion in London, British Library (**GB**-Lbl), Lansdowne 763 (mid-fifteenth century), f. 123^{v}: "proporcionum quedam sunt pronunciative quedam denunciative. Proporciones denunciative pertinent ad Geometriam Astronomiam Arithmetricam. & Musicam speculativam. Proporciones pronunciative pertinent ad Musicam practicam scilicet ad Cantores [Certain proportions are performative, others are descriptive. Descriptive proportions pertain to Geometry, Astronomy, Arithmetic, and Speculative Music. Performative proportions pertain to Practical Music, that is, to singers]."

[7]Margaret Bent, "Notation, §III, 3: Polyphonic Mensural Notation, *c*1260–1500," in *The New Grove Dictionary of Music and Musicians*, 2d ed. [hereafter *NGD*], 29 vols., ed. Stanley Sadie (London: Macmillan, 2001), 18:136; Anna Maria Busse Berger, *Mensuration and Proportion Signs: Origins and Evolution* (Oxford: Clarendon Press; New York: Oxford University Press, 1993), 164.

[8]On these developments, see Berger, *Mensuration and Proportion Signs*, especially 164–82.

For much of the fourteenth and early fifteenth centuries, at least, English theorists and practitioners were in the closest alignment with international developments. It is revealing that in such a comprehensive work as the *Quatuor principalia* (mid-fourteenth century), the material explaining proportions is limited to the discussion of intervals at the close of the second *principale*, while the fourth *principale* (on mensural music) lacks a rhythmic application of proportions.[9] At the slightly later period when free proportional treatment became a regularly available feature of contrapuntal composition, the situation changed, and in English writings of the early fifteenth century onwards, we find demonstrations of proportions in practical use. The addition of the modern element of rhythmic proportionality and mensural examples remained, nevertheless, just that: an addition grafted onto the traditional (purely arithmetical) teaching of proportions, and this holds equally true for the major continental expositions from Prosdocimus onward.[10]

The examples of the treatise beginning *Pars aliquota est* show a full awareness of current practices, employing numerals and mensuration signs as indicators of proportions; this discussion is one of the earliest expositions of "practical" rhythmic proportions anywhere in Europe.[11] Among the various discussions of proportions in London, British Library (**GB**-Lbl), Lansdowne 763, including the well-known treatise of Chilston,[12] a single exposition (ending the manuscript) offers examples in mensural notation.[13] This short treatise demonstrates six basic proportions that are held to be in

[9]Principale 2, chaps. 20–24; edited and translated in Luminita Florea Aluas, "The *Quatuor principalia musicae*: A Critical Edition and Translation, with Introduction and Commentary" (Ph.D. dissertation, Indiana University, 1996), 249–56; and *Scriptorum de musica medii aevi nova series a Gerbertina altera*, 4 vols., ed. Edmond de Coussemaker (Paris: Durand, 1864–76; reprint, Hildesheim: Olms, 1963), 4:216–19.

[10]In this light, the various English manuscript "clusters" of proportion texts need to be considered as representatives a single larger tradition, even when the majority of the individual texts treat only the mathematical material. Such sets of writings are to be found in Rome, Biblioteca Apostolica Vaticana (**I**-Rvat), Reg. lat. 1146; **GB**-Lbl Lansdowne 763; New York, Pierpont Morgan Library (**US**-NYpm), B 12; and Oxford, Bodleian Library (**GB**-Ob), Bodley 842.

[11]**I**-Rvat Reg. lat. 1146, ff. 48^{r}–51^{r}; Berger, *Mensuration and Proportion Signs*, 183, n. 77. Although this manuscript has traditionally been dated to the fourteenth century, Berger assigns *Pars aliquota est* to the early fifteenth century, probably based on the advanced treatment of the subject matter (*Mensuration and Proportion Signs*, 58, 66, 166, and 177).

[12]Ff. 117^{r}–122^{v}; edited in Sanford B. Meech, "Three Musical Treatises in English from a Fifteenth-Century Manuscript," *Speculum* 10 (1935): 265–69.

[13]Ff. 123^{v}–124^{r}.

practical use,[14] with extremely brief two-voice examples in which the higher voice remains in diminution against the tenor throughout. For signalling the proportions intended in each example, an inconsistent selection of mensuration signs, Hindu-Arabic numerals (2 and 4 only), or no sign whatsoever is applied. In general character (and contrapuntal crudity), these compositions offer a precedent for another set of unpublished and barely acknowledged proportional examples in the theory section of the manuscript Cambridge, Magdalene College (**GB**-Cmc), Pepys 1236 (ca. 1465–75).[15] Considerably more garbled in transmission or composition than the earlier sets,[16] the proportional examples from the Pepys manuscript again employ no consistent notational system to indicate which proportions are intended; readers are served best by the proportion names written near the examples (where these are correct).

Slightly later than the Pepys book, the theory miscellany **GB**-Lbl Additional 10336 (the notebook of John Tucke, compiled probably during the first two decades of the sixteenth century) includes various texts dealing with proportions, among them a unique treatise by John Hothby.[17] The English Carmelite, whose writings are preserved mainly in Italian sources, left behind several proportion treatises that are purely mathematical works; the section expounding the theory of proportions from his treatise in **GB**-

---

[14] These are *dupla*, *tripla*, *quadrupla*, *sesquialtera*, *sesquitertia*, and *sesquioctava*, a limited set that is absolutely typical of this stage of the theory; see Berger, *Mensuration and Proportion Signs*, 167.

[15] Ff. 107^{v}–108^{v}. Woodley characterizes these pieces as "a sequence of interesting, though highly implausible, polyphonic examples of proportion" (*John Tucke*, 99, n. 67). The similarities between the Discant voices in the *tripla* examples of **GB**-Lbl Lansdowne 763 and Cambridge, Magdalene College (**GB**-Cmc), Pepys 1236 suggests that there is more than a general stylistic link between the two sets.

[16] Note, for example, the demonstrations of the nonsensical proportions "subsesquitercia biparciens 9as" and "Quadriparciens octauas" (the latter of which, even with the more correct title *superquadriparciens octauas*, as 12:8 would be an example of *sesquialtera*; moreover, the example demonstrates simple *octupla*).

[17] On the dating of the gradual compilation of the manuscript, see Woodley, *John Tucke*, 63–65. I follow Woodley in considering Reaney's *Regule cantus mensurati secundum Ioannem Otteby* (*Johannes Hothby, Opera omnia de musica mensurabili; Thomas Walsingham, Regulae de musica mensurabili*, ed. Gilbert Reaney, Corpus scriptorum de musica, vol. 31 [Neuhausen-Stuttgart: Hänssler Verlag for the American Institute of Musicology, 1983], 51–59) to be part of a single treatise beginning *Quid est proportio* (Woodley, *John Tucke*, 50–52); if these are to be treated as separate works, the explicit to the *Regule* calling it *Proportiones secundum Joannem Otteby* certainly makes little sense, and there would be no reason to attribute *Quid est proportio* to Hothby. Another English copy of the treatise survives in **GB**-Llp 466, but this manuscript is mainly a direct copy of Tucke's book made in 1526 (Woodley, *John Tucke*, 65).

Lbl Add. 10336 is among these non-musical discussions.[18] In the section of the treatise dealing with rhythmic divisions under various mensurations, we find (alongside a complex and unusual extension of the system of mensuration signs) the notation of a set of signs meant to designate six basic proportions: ⊍, Ͽ, ⩀, ∪, Ɔ, and ∩ as *sesquialtera, subsesquitertia, sesquioctava, subsesquialtera, sesquitertia*, and *subsesquioctava*.[19] Such a system, which can only be related in a vague manner to the usages actually encountered in the practical sources,[20] is not significant because of the details of its seemingly arbitrary connections between sign and proportion. Rather, the attempt here to construct a symbolic shorthand notation for proportions represents one of a number of such experiments encountered in English sources—another of which is presented in the second treatise edited in the present volume. The use of unusual permutations and combinations of mensuration signs as notational markers for proportions, probably a delayed continuation from and development on the experiments of ca. 1400,[21] can be observed in a text from the Tucke manuscript whose system bears a direct relation to the second Dygon treatise.[22]

An alternative approach to proportional notation in several fifteenth- and early sixteenth-century English texts, again probably an unusual and mainly speculative development out of fourteenth-century notational innovations, is the use of a wide palette of colors with individual proportional meanings. Appearing in texts from **GB**-Lbl Lansdowne 763 and Cambridge, Corpus Christi College (**GB**-Ccc), 410/II (second half of the fifteenth century) and, most explicitly, in Tucke's famous notebook, the employment of colors beyond black and red to notate passages in unusual proportions could have provided early Tudor composers with a vehicle to place their learning on display, according to certain scholars. The surviving musical sources

---

[18]The proportion section of the treatise (beginning "Quid est proportio," f. 58^r, ending with proportion tables on f. 62^{r-v}) remains unedited. For editions of the other proportion treatises, see *Johannes Hothby, Opera omnia de proportionibus; Anonymus, Tractatus de contrapunto (Ms. Venice, Lat. VIII.82, coll. 3047)*, ed. Gilbert Reaney, Corpus scriptorum de musica, vol. 39 (Neuhausen-Stuttgart: Hänssler Verlag for the American Institute of Musicology, 1997).

[19]Ff. 67^v–68^r; *Johannes Hothby, Opera omnia de musica mensurabili* (ed. Reaney), 54.

[20]The only one of these signs encountered in other sources with the meaning given here is Ɔ as *sesquitertia*.

[21]See the examples listed in Berger, *Mensuration and Proportion Signs*, 170–76.

[22]See pp. 53–56 *infra*.

nevertheless provide nothing more extreme than two early fifteenth-century examples of blue notation.[23]

These idiosyncratic approaches to proportional signification have in common the fact that their effect on general practice could have been extremely limited at best, to judge from the musical sources. A single late sixteenth-century manuscript (Baldwin's Commonplace Book [**GB**-Lbl R.M. 24.d.2]) demonstrates a variety of combinations of mensuration signs in connection with proportions that recalls the earlier experiments—but even there, any discernible system is extremely inconsistent and the reader must rely on the verbal and numerical proportional designations written nearby.[24] Single mensuration signs as well as sign-numeral combinations (not "modus cum tempore" signs, however) and numerals (single or in pairs)—usually accompanied by coloration—serve to signify simple proportions such as *tripla* and *sesquialtera* in the York mass fragments;[25] this usage connects only in a loose and indirect way to some of the single-symbol proportional notations mentioned above. The more usual situation in the English sources of the later fifteenth and early sixteenth centuries, however, is a more standard and systematic proportional notation. The frequent appearance of *sesquialtera* (3:2) passages in the Eton Choirbook (Windsor, Eton College Library [**GB**-WRec], 178) is marked in most cases both by a switch from black full to red full notation (the standard *sesquialtera* coloration at binary rhythmic levels) and by the written numerals "3 2." The same coloration pattern (black full-red full) obtains in the Fayrfax Manuscript (**GB**-Lbl Additional 5465), but with only the numeral 3; and in the "Henry VIII Manuscript" (**GB**-Lbl Additional 31922), where simple black coloration with the numeral 3 is in line with contemporaneous continental habit.[26]

---

[23]For the hypothesis of early-Tudor polychromatic notation, see Woodley, *John Tucke*, 68–75 and 110–21; Roger Bray, "Music and the Quadrivium in Early Tudor England," *Music and Letters* 76 (1995): 2–4 and 12–14; and idem, "Editing and Performing *Musica Speculativa*,'" in *English Choral Practice, 1400–1650*, ed. John Morehen (Cambridge: Cambridge University Press, 1995), 54. Both examples of blue notation are found in the Old Hall Manuscript (**GB**-Lbl Additional 57950).

[24]See figure 2 and p. 53 *infra*.

[25]York, Borthwick Institute of Historical Research (**GB**-Ybi), Mus. 1, e.g., ff. 5^v–6^r and 10^v–11^r.

[26]In the notation of both numbers, if not in the combination of coloration and numerals, the Eton scribe was actually closer to Tinctoris's recommendations than most continental scribes, for whom the single numeral 3 usually sufficed—much to the theorist's annoyance. The combination of coloration and a single numeral found in **GB**-Lbl Additional 31922 and **GB**-Lbl Additional 5465 was exactly that for which Tinctoris had once criticized Busnoys, although the use of coloration in addition to the numeral was less in use in the early sixteenth century. Johannes Tinctoris, *Proportionale musices*, Lib. 3, Cap. 2;

For more advanced proportional passages in the Forrest-Heyther Partbooks (**GB**-Ob Mus. Sch. e.376-81), as in Baldwin's book, the appearance of the names of proportions alongside pairs of Hindu-Arabic numerals testifies to a goal of erudite display as well as didactic purposes; but the use of numerals is the essential aspect of the notation.[27]

In these "mainstream" cases of proportional notation from the practical sources, there is a disconnection from most of the notational systems described in the English theoretical writings up to the early sixteenth century. From the musical examples of rhythmic proportions in the treatises, as well as the written descriptions of symbols connected to proportions, there is little indication that English theorists prior to Dygon were interested in the conceptually simple and infinitely extensible system of proportional notation described by Prosdocimus and demonstrated more fully in the writings of Tinctoris and Gaffurius—that is, the indication of each proportion through a pair of Hindu-Arabic numerals. In an arithmetic context (or in the context of *musica speculativa* writings), Hindu-Arabic numerals were being used with ever greater consistency in the fourteenth and fifteenth centuries, and treatments of rhythmic values such as the triangle diagrams in music theory manuscripts employed such numerals from their appearance in the fourteenth century.[28] The appearance of Hindu-Arabic numerals for convenience in texts and diagrams, however, seems not to have led the English theorists to describe their systematic use as elements of music notation. It is striking that a printed continental treatise first prompted an English writer to set out the idea at home—in the first of the two treatises edited here—and in all likelihood at a time when native musical sources

---

Lib. 1, Cap. 6; Lib. 3, Cap. 4; in *Opera theoretica*, 3 vols. in 2, ed. Albert Seay, Corpus scriptorum de musica, vol. 22 (n.p.: American Institute of Musicology, 1975–78), 2a:44–45, 2a:19–20, and 2a:52.

[27]For a discussion of some instances of proportional notation in the Forrest-Heyther Partbooks, see Woodley, *John Tucke*, 112–21.

[28]For several examples of the triangle (attributed to Torkesey or Brunham and appearing in many variant versions), see **GB**-Ctc O.9.29, ff. 53v–54v; **GB**-Lbl Additional 21455, ff. 7r–8v; **GB**-Ob Bodley 515, f. 2r–v. A basic edition can be found in *Breviarium regulare musicae*, ed. Gilbert Reaney; *Tractatus de figuris sive de notis*, ed. Gilbert Reaney; *Johannes Torkesey, Declaratio trianguli et scuti*, ed. André Gilles and Gilbert Reaney, Corpus scriptorum de musica, vol. 12 (n.p.: American Institute of Musicology, 1966), 58–61. That the appearance of Hindu-Arabic numerals in these diagrams considerably predates their use in practical music sources may be significant for historical developments, but it must be emphasized that their use of numerals derives from their arithmetical, learned context, related to other academic texts; the notational developments in the musical sources follow a different track.

already showed an awareness of the practice.[29] Furthermore, the more original second treatise in the Cambridge manuscript, while repeating the Gaffurian structure of the first treatise, has as its purpose the extension of a particularly English system for notating proportions with combinations of mensuration signs.[30] In the second Dygon treatise, thus, a process of Anglicization transforms a continental original and arrives at yet another theoretical notation system that would remain divorced from practice.

The details of the system of notation, however, are not the only aspects of Dygon's treatises in which an English view was grafted onto Gaffurius's text. Instances of interjections relating to practical issues represent the concerns of the English musician and will be discussed in the close examination of the treatises below. A significant example is Dygon's important theoretical corroboration for a proportional practice described in Thomas Morley's famous *Plaine and easie introduction to practicall musicke*, which is the use of *inductiones proportionum*. This operation involves the use of a common proportion to lead into another for ease of performance, such as when a composer writes a brevis's worth of *sesquialtera* or *tripla* to introduce a *sextupla* section.[31] Morley actually criticized the technique, wondering "that a thing which neither is of any use, nor yet can be proved by any reason, should so much be stood upon by them who take upon them to teach the youth nowadays."[32] Morley's complaint, along with Dygon's insertion of an explanation of *inductiones* into Gaffurius's text, suggests that the practice was an English (or British) one, a view confirmed in Richard Pace's *De fructu qui ex doctrina percipitur* (printed in 1517 and ostensibly written for the edification of boys at St. Paul's School). Ending a discussion of the medical "diesis arteriae," Pace exhibits a certain nationalistic pride in mentioning the invention of *inductiones* by British *musici*:

---

[29]On the possible dating of the Dygon treatises, see pp. 57–64 *infra*. Sources from the years around 1500 such as the Eton Choirbook and the Fayrfax Manuscript almost certainly predate the treatises in **GB**-Ctc O.3.38.

[30]See pp. 48–57 *infra*.

[31]For a detailed explanation, see pp. 34–36 *infra*.

[32]Thomas Morley, *A Plain and Easy Introduction to Practical Music*, ed. R. Alec Harman, 2d ed. (London: J. M. Dent; New York: W. W. Norton, 1963), 136.

… sed si Galenus eam re uera deprehendit, illum non imperitiorem musices, quam artis medicae fuisse iudico. Est enim haec res quamsimillima illi subtilitati, quam musici acutissime indagarunt in proportionum suarum inductionibus. Dissident & musici inter se, & quidem subtiliter. Aliqui unius consonantiae suauitatem & perfectionem, aliqui alterius extollentes. tum uero, quod difficilius est, rationem huius rei indagantes, quam haud dubie musici huius temporis non sunt inuenturi, nisi graece docti, ad bibliothecam summi Pontificis accedant, ubi (ut dictum est) multi sunt in re musica optimi libri. Ceterum hoc ausim dicere, nostros Britannos musicos, maxima ingenij subtilitate (si quis acutius rem introspiciat) illas quas uocant proportionum inductiones, inuenisse, & hac una re omnem antiquitatem superasse. Sed e diuerso illud miror, magnam partem illorum nescire quod sciunt, & scire quod nesciunt.[33]

… But if Galen really detected it, I think he knew as much about music as he did about the art of medicine. For this's [*sic*] very similar to the subtle distinctions musicians try hard to make in the inductions of their proportions.

Musicians also disagree among themselves, and subtly at that. Some extol the sweetness and perfection of one consonance, others of another. Then, with greater difficulty, they search for reasons for their opinion, which they're never going to find unless they know Greek. They can go to the Vatican Library where, as I've mentioned, there're many excellent books on music. Yet I dare say, if one looks into it closely, our British musicians have found with great subtlety of mind those things they call the inductions of proportions, and in that one thing they've surpassed all antiquity. But on the other hand, I'm amazed that most of them do not know what they know and know what they do not know.

Pace was in a particularly good position to compare British and continental musical practices, having been sent to the University of Padua by Thomas Langton, Bishop of Winchester, on account of his musical skill as a boy. During a period in Rome in the service of Cardinal Bainbridge, from 1509 to 1514, the famed humanist took the opportunity to study music treatises in the Vatican Library; his own testimony is one of the first explicit evidences of English contact with foreign music theory in the Tudor period, a phenomenon that would only increase in frequency and significance.[34]

[33] Richard Pace, *De fructu qui ex doctrina percipitur (The Benefit of a Liberal Education)*, ed. and trans. Frank Manley and Richard S. Sylvester (New York: Ungar, 1967), 64–67. I have modified the translation slightly to render technical terms with their standard English equivalents.

[34] Ibid., 38–39 and 46–47. See also Theodor Dumitrescu, "Anglo-Continental Musical Relations, *c.* 1485–1530," 2 vols. (D.Phil. thesis, University of Oxford, 2004), 1:18–22; a revised version of this thesis is forthcoming as *The Early Tudor Court and International Musical Relations* (Aldershot: Ashgate, in press).

The use of continental music treatises as models for British writing in the sixteenth century can be seen as one element in a larger complex of foreign influences throughout the century.[35] Already at the end of the fifteenth century, Henry VII's gradual expansions to the musical establishment at the royal court were bringing more instrumentalists from the Continent into permanent English employment than ever before, alongside numerous foreign scholars and artists. With the accession of Henry VIII, who had been brought up in an increasingly international environment, this hiring trend continued unabated, and for much of his reign foreigners represented a major portion of the royal instrumental musicians. These trends in the royal households, reflected occasionally by noble employers, resulted as well in the immigration of composers who would have a considerable impact on sixteenth-century English musical life, such as Benedictus de Opiciis, Philip van Wilder, Derick Gerarde, and Alfonso Ferrabosco. The musical sources themselves reflect this situation, with an initial influx of foreign-made manuscripts (and the occasional print) in the early sixteenth century gradually leading to the integration of continental music into native sources.

The situation was similar for the tradition of music theory, although here a greater scarcity of sources discourages firm conclusions. Certain writings from the late fifteenth and early sixteenth centuries, such as the descriptions of compositional devices in **GB**-Lbl Add. 10336 and the theory section of **GB**-Cmc Pepys 1236, seem to represent an idiosyncratic English approach to music theory,[36] although John Hothby, as the foremost English theorist of the fifteenth century, probably spent the majority of his musical career teaching in Italy and could well have provided a conduit for the transmission of musical ideas between England and continental Europe.[37] With the rise of printed music treatises, examples of large-scale theoretical writings from the Continent began to enter England from the first decades of the sixteenth century. The bookseller John Dorne in Oxford, upon returning from a journey across the channel in August 1520, sold two exemplars of Nicolaus Wollick's *Opus aureum musicae* (Cologne: Heinrich Quentell, 1501) as well as a copy of Andreas Ornithoparcus's *Musice active micrologus* (Leipzig:

---

[35]This broader issue is investigated in Dumitrescu, "Anglo-Continental Musical Relations."

[36]On this style of theoretical writing, see Woodley, *John Tucke.*

[37]Currently accepted musicological views tend to consider Hothby's teachings as consequential only for continental practice (cf. Woodley, *John Tucke*, vii); for indications of Hothby's influence in England, however, see Dumitrescu, "Anglo-Continental Musical Relations," 1:204–6 and 221–23.

Valentin Schumann, 1517);[38] the latter work is still known to the English-speaking world mainly through John Dowland's translation printed in 1609. We can find occasional marks of sixteenth-century English ownership in surviving volumes, such as the marginalia and additions on blank pages in **GB**-Ob 4° W 9 (2) Art. Seld., combining Michael Koswick's *Compendiaria musice artis aeditio* (Leipzig: Wolffgang Stöckel, 1516) with Wollick's *Enchiridion musices* (Paris: Jehan Petit et François Regnault, 1512).[39] For the present study, it is significant that at least two of the copies of Gaffurius's *Practica musice* preserved in the British Library, both from the 1502 Brescian printing, may have been in England from an early date: **GB**-Lbl 59.d.20 comes from the Old Royal Library (but not the library of Henry Fitzalan, which introduced many music books into the royal collection)[40] and **GB**-Lbl K.1.g.5 was presented to the British Museum by John Hawkins in 1778, according to a note on a flyleaf. The extensive marginalia entered into the latter book by the eighteenth-century writer, however, obscure the presence of another set of additions by a distinctly English sixteenth-century hand in appearance, which is particularly clear in Book IV, the source for Dygon's treatises.

The effect that the treatises in **GB**-Ctc O.3.38 might have had on later English theory is particularly difficult to gauge. In the few surviving treatises by British authors from later in the sixteenth century, Gaffurius's printed *Practica musice* acts as an important source, apparently without intermediate stages of transmission such as Dygon's book. The anonymous Scottish author of **GB**-Lbl Additional 4911, writing probably around 1580, used Gaffurius's treatise as the main model for the structure of his own, in addition to quoting and adapting portions of the Italian book and other major works by continental theorists (for example, Wollick, Georg Rhaw, Hermann Finck, and Martin Agricola).[41] Morley's *Plaine and easie intro-*

[38]Dietrich Helms, *Heinrich VIII. und die Musik* (Eisenach: Wagner, 1998), 424–25. Helms suggests as well that a "p^r^intyd musyke boke" in the will of Henry Turton (1533), being listed separately from "all my pryksonge bookis of masse antemes and sqwares," was probably a theory book (ibid., 174 and 442); a similar possibility exists for the "boke of musyk in latyn" in a post-mortem inventory (1538) of the goods of the printer John Rastell (ibid., 166, n. 38 and 440).

[39]The handwritten additions include the name of Thomas Morley, as well as notes in a hand and style of orthography that would date them to the mid-sixteenth century, e.g., "6 4 ys sesqualtra" at the end of the Koswick treatise.

[40]Helms, *Heinrich VIII.*, 181–82.

[41]See Judson Maynard, "An Anonymous Scottish Treatise on Music from the Sixteenth Century, British Museum Additional Manuscript 4911, Edition and Commentary," 2 vols. (Ph.D. dissertation, Indiana University, 1961), especially 1:5–7, 40, 76, 79, 148,

duction similarly includes Gaffurius among the numerous "late writers" whose books the Englishman consulted; in terms of specifically British practices, his comments on the *inductiones* and the example match those of Dygon closely.[42] The sources informing the other major English books, William Bathe's *Briefe Introduction* of ca. 1587 and the anonymous *Pathway to musicke* printed in London in 1596, are unnamed and less certain, though in the case of the latter, Morley's sarcastic criticisms include the information that the material for the treatise was "filched out of" Lossius, Beurhusius, and one other book.[43] Dygon's treatises are neither cited nor quoted by the late sixteenth-century authors and cannot be shown to have been a direct influence, but they certainly represent one aspect of a cohesive earlier theoretical tradition out of which the later compendia grew.

In the centuries since Dygon's book passed out of relevance for contemporary practice, the volume has received little attention. The short passage in John Hawkins's *A General History of the Science and Practice of Music* concerning Dygon contains a transcription of one of his compositions from Baldwin's Commonplace Book but no mention of the theoretical work. Similarly, W. H. Grattan Flood does not seem to have been aware of the treatises when writing his *Early Tudor Composers*, which otherwise gathered the details of Dygon's life then known.[44] Discussion of the treatises is

---

and 160; and on the origin of the manuscript, Isobel P. Woods, "A Note on 'Scottish Anonymous,'" *Royal Music Association Research Chronicle* 21 (1988): 37–39. With regard to the issue of whether the Scottish treatise has any relevance to English music, note that the author (whose examples include a fair amount of English polyphony) qualifies certain non-continental practices as British, rather than Scottish or English (see, for example, Maynard, "An Anonymous Scottish Treatise," 2:13–14 and 21–25).

[42]Morley, *A Plain and Easy Introduction* (ed. Harman), 319; pp. 34–35 *infra.*

[43]William Bathe, *A Briefe Introduction to the Skill of Song* (London: Thomas Este, [ca. 1587]; reprint, with introduction by Bernarr Rainbow, Kilkenny: Boethius Press, 1982); *The Pathway to Musicke* (London: William Barley, 1596); Morley, *A Plain and Easy Introduction* (ed. Harman), 130–31. The section of the *Pathway* on discant, which Morley says the author "took verbatim out of an old written book which I have," seems to be the last source to recommend the use of sights, a mainly English technique for visualizing counterpoints on the same staff as a *cantus firmus.* The process is described in the English counterpoint manuals of the fourteenth and fifteenth centuries and mentioned by certain continental writers of the later fifteenth century, but disappears thereafter; see Dumitrescu, "Anglo-Continental Musical Relations," 1:194–203.

[44]John Hawkins, *A General History of the Science and Practice of Music*, 5 vols. (London: T. Payne & Son, 1776; reprint, London: Novello, 1853), 356–58; W. H. Grattan Flood, *Early Tudor Composers: Biographical Sketches of Thirty-Two Musicians and Composers of the Period 1485–1555* (London: Oxford University Press, 1925), 104–7. On Dygon's compositions, see pp. 22–23 *infra.*

completely absent from certain investigations into Tudor music theory,[45] although the manuscript appears in the standard catalogues.[46] The Cambridge manuscript was presumably a source for Emden's identification of Dygon with John "Vuylborus," using an orthography of the latter name found in the treatise.[47] Thurston Dart used Dygon's assertion that *sextupla* at the level of the minima was too quick for fingers or lips as a confirmation of instrumental performance of counterpoint in mensural notation.[48] Only with the publication of Rufus Hallmark's brief notice concerning the manuscript did Dygon's use of Gaffurius's text became known; that article has remained until now the sole published study of the book.[49]

The Author of the Treatises

The identification of the redactor of the writings in **GB**-Ctc O.3.38 with John Dygon is based on an inscription found at the end of the first treatise, reading "Qd' Joannes Dygonus M° Vuylborus." The assertion in *The New Grove Dictionary of Music and Musicians* that the treatise "has been ascribed to Dygon on the strength of a note following a music example" is misleading: the phrase clearly stands at the end of the first of the book's two major sections, with the remainder of the page left blank, as well as the

---

[45]For example, Bray, "Music and Musicians"; and Woodley, *John Tucke.*

[46]M. R. James, *The Western Manuscripts in the Library of Trinity College, Cambridge: A Descriptive Catalogue*, 4 vols. (Cambridge: Cambridge University Press, 1900–1904), 3:220–21; Christian Meyer, Michel Huglo, and Nancy C. Phillips, *The Theory of Music: Manuscripts from the Carolingian Era up to c.1500 in Great Britain and in the United States of America*, RISM BIII/4 (Munich: Henle, 1992), 8–9.

[47]Alfred Brotherston Emden, *A Biographical Register of the University of Oxford, A.D. 1501 to 1540* (Oxford: Clarendon Press, 1974), 182. The issue of Dygon's identity is discussed below.

[48]Thurston Dart, "Origines et sources de la musique de chambre en Angleterre (1500–1530)," in *La musique instrumentale de la Renaissance*, ed. Jean Jacquot (Paris: Centre Nationale de la Recherche Scientifique, 1955), 82. Passing references to the manuscript also appear in Andrew Wathey, "Notes on Discant and Mensuration from Fifteenth-Century Oxford," in *Trent'anni di ricerca musicologica: Studi in onore di F. Alberto Gallo*, ed. Patrizia Dalla Vecchia and Donatella Restani (Rome: Torre d'Orfeo, 1996), 66; and Helms, *Heinrich VIII.*, 164 n. 31.

[49]Rufus Hallmark, "An Unknown English Treatise." See also Dumitrescu, "Anglo-Continental Musical Relations," 1:210–17. Frank Ll. Harrison offers a brief description of the manuscript's contents in "Music at Oxford before 1500," in *The History of the University of Oxford*, vol. 2, *Late Medieval Oxford*, ed. J. I. Catto and Ralph Evans (Oxford: Clarendon Press, 1992; reprint, 1995), 358.

entire following page.[50] The formula "Quod [N.]" appears to be a peculiarly English usage and is not necessarily meant to suggest authorship in the modern sense.[51] Nor is the phrase a mere indication of scribal activity, and in the present case Dygon can be considered to be the editor of the texts in the book and composer of the examples (with the exception of the two copied from Gaffurius).

Dygon was a Benedictine and prior of St. Augustine's monastery in Canterbury from 1528 until the abbey's dissolution in July 1538.[52] We can be certain that it was this man who was responsible for the treatises (and not, for example, the John Dygon who was abbot of St. Augustine's from 1497 to 1509[53]) on account of the ascription of several short compositions in John Baldwin's Commonplace Book to "m^r^ iohn digon prior of s^t^ augustines," as well as other references to be discussed below.[54] Dygon was at St. Augustine's by March 1505 (when he was ordained subdeacon, becoming a deacon in April 1506) and supplicated for the B.Mus. at the University of Oxford on 28 March 1512. It seems unlikely that the John Dygon who took a civil law degree at Oxford in 1533 is the same man, but the monk enjoyed at least one further period of study. Having made Dygon sub-prior of St. Augustine's in 1521, the abbot John Essex (*alias* Foche) allowed the musician around this time to travel to the Continent along with Nicholas Wotton, where they studied at the Universities of Leuven and Paris with the famed humanist Juan Luis Vives. This information derives from the Canterbury antiquarian John Twyne's *De rebus albionicis*, first

[50] Stanley Boorman with Roger Bowers, "Dygon, John," in *NGD*, 7:816. The inscription is on f. 12r. See plate 1, p. 171 *infra*.

[51] See, for example, the statement "quod J. Wylde" at the end of the "Regule Magistri Johannis de Muris" on f. 98r of **GB**-Lbl Lansdowne 763, or "quod Alex" at the end of the copy of Robert Grosseteste's Commentary on Aristotle's *Posterior Analytics* in **GB**-Ob Lat. Misc. d.83 (Wathey, "Notes on discant," 64). The phrase "quod Beche nomen scriptoris Gallicus plenus amoris" at the end of the *Regimen animarum* in a mid-fourteenth-century English codex seems to indicate activity as both scribe and compiler (see Thomas J. Mathiesen, "'The Office of the New Feast of Corpus Christi' in the *Regimen Animarum* at Brigham Young University," *Journal of Musicology* 2 [1983]: 17–18). Many further English examples of the formula exist.

[52] A brief overview of Dygon's appointments appears in Emden, *A Biographical Register*, 182; see also Boorman, "Dygon, John."

[53] According to the entry in Emden's *Biographical Register*, this man was the uncle of the younger John Dygon; the source for the information is unspecified.

[54] **GB**-Lbl R.M. 24.d.2, ff. 165v–166r; available in facsimile as *London, British Library, R.M. 24.d.2*, facsimile edition with introduction by Jessie Ann Owens, Renaissance Music in Facsimile, vol. 8 (New York: Garland, 1987). These pieces are discussed further on pp. 22–23 *infra* and edited in the Appendix.

published posthumously in 1590, which reports as well that the two students returned to England in the company of the Spanish scholar (therefore in 1523).[55] Dygon's last promotion was to prior of the abbey in the late 1520s.

From the final years of St. Augustine's and the period after its dissolution, the concrete remnants of Dygon's activities are accompanied by the confused traces of several possible identities for the musician under different names. A single letter from Dygon survives, written in English to Lord Lisle at the beginning of 1534/5 concerning the latter's recommendation of a Thomas Upryse.[56] For the sake of comparison, the signature at the end of this letter is reproduced in figure 1, alongside the specimen of Dygon's signature from the deed of surrender for St. Augustine's (30 July 1538) and the ascription to Dygon in **GB**-Ctc O.3.38.[57] The first two are in a different and less formal style of script than that employed for the formula naming Dygon in **GB**-Ctc O.3.38, as seen in figure 1c, preventing any firm conclusions about the identification of the hand in the theory manuscript with Dygon's.

In the lists of pensions granted to the monks of St. Augustine's after its dissolution, the name of John Dygon does not appear. The accounts of the Court of Augmentations show that the members of the late monastery were pensioned on 3 September 1538, just over a month after the deed of surrender was drawn up.[58] A comparison of names between the signatures on the deed of surrender and the first pension list reveals that of the thirty monks (excluding the abbot), all but three changed their surnames.[59] Abbot Essex

[55]John Twyne, *De rebus Albionicis, Britannicis atque Anglicis, commentariorum libri duo* (London: Edm. Bollifantus, pro Richardo Watkins, 1590), 6–7. Dygon's name does not appear in the matriculation lists from Leuven during this period, published in *Matricule de l'Université de Louvain*, ed. Arnold Schillings, E. H. J. Reusens, and Joseph Wils, 10 vols. in 18, Académie royale des sciences, des lettres et des beaux-arts de Belgique, Commission royale d'histoire, [Publications in-quarto], vol. 35 (Brussels: Kiessling, 1903–80); matriculation, however, was not necessarily a prerequisite to study at a university.

[56]London, Public Record Office (**GB**-Lpro SP3/3), no. 21; calendared in *Letters and Papers, Foreign and Domestic, of the Reign of Henry VIII*, ed. J. S. Brewer et al., 2d ed. (London: H. M. Stationery Office, 1920), Addenda 1/1, no. 976.

[57]**GB**-Lpro E322/49; calendared in *Letters and Papers* 13/1, no. 1503.

[58]**GB**-Lpro E315/232; calendared in *Letters and Papers* 14/1, no. 1355, Book 232/II, fols. 65^v–71^r. The pension for Abbot Essex is recorded in Book 233, f. 141^v.

[59]Any doubt that the two lists refer to exactly the same set of monks is dispelled by the complete correlation between the numbers of first names: 1 David, 2 Edwards, 1 George, 9 Johns, 1 Lawrence, 1 Ralph, 2 Richards, 4 Roberts, 3 Thomases, 6 Williams. The three who retained their names were David Franklin, George Amys, and William Burgys.

does not appear on the September list, his much larger pension and grant being awarded in February. Although the name Dygon is missing, the recipient of the final and highest pension listed is the previously unknown "John Wyldebere," with £13 6*s* 8*d*.[60] Of the thirty monks on the original pension list, sixteen were still alive and receiving their pensions in 1556, appearing in Cardinal Pole's comprehensive list of pensions in England and Wales; the final name on the list is still "Johannes Wilborne," with the same pension of £13 6*s* 8*d*.[61]

a. London, Public Record Office (**GB**-Lpro) SP3/3, no. 21 ("John dygon p*ri*or")

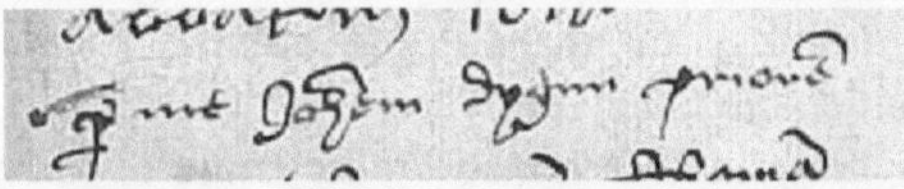

b. **GB**-Lpro E322/49 ("p*er* me Joh*ann*em dygun prior*em*")

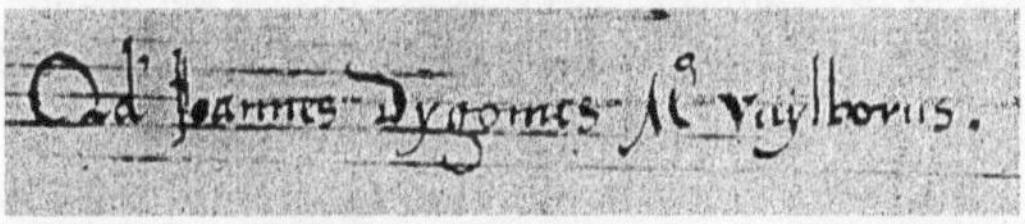

c. **GB**-Ctc O.3.38, f. 12^{r} ("Q*uo*d Joannes Dygonus M*odo* Vuylborus")

Figure 1

The implication of these documents, that Dygon (as former prior) is to be identified with John Wilborne, has been a matter of concern since the earliest efforts at tracing the composer's biography. The appearance of both names in **GB**-Ctc O.3.38 has not previously resolved the issue, since the reading of the inscription as "Q[uo]d Joannes Dygonus M[agisṭr]o Vuylborns" would indicate that "Wylborns" (in the dative) is the dedicatee or recipient and "Dygonus" is the creator of the work.[62] This reading of the

[60]**GB**-Lpro E315/232, f. 71^{r}.

[61]**GB**-Lpro E164/31, f. 3^{v}.

[62]No published discussion of the inscription expands this abbreviation. The entry in RISM BIII/4 clearly follows the "Magistro" interpretation: "Il [*sc.* Dygon] a offert ou écrit ce traité pour le maître Wybbors" (p. 8).

text is surely faulty, however: the standard expansion of the abbreviation "M°" should be "Modo," which here would have the sense of "now"—in other words, the inscription refers to the musician's change of name from Dygon to Wylbore ("*Quod* John Dygon, now Wylbore").[63] Furthermore, another surviving document confirms conclusively that the two names were in fact used by one man: the archiepiscopal register of Thomas Cranmer, Archbishop of Canterbury, records that on 23 June 1545 the perpetual vicarage of the parish church of Preston was granted to "magistrum Iohanem Wyldebore alias Dygon sacre theologie bacc."[64] The wording of this source leaves little room for dispute, offering an explicit identification of Wylbore and Dygon as well as the new information that he was the holder of a bachelor's degree in theology.

From the historical documentation, then, it would appear certain that Dygon began using the name Wylbore immediately following the dissolution of St. Augustine's, the switch occurring between 30 July and 3 September 1538. What reason can he have had for taking up the name? The practice was certainly widespread at the Dissolution and leads to a confusing documentary picture: as F. A. Gasquet notes, "the difficulty of identifying the religious at this time is very considerable. They are variously described by their Christian, religious, or surnames, and often also by the name of their birthplace."[65] The example of Abbot Essex of St. Augustine's provides a case in point, since in addition to the names Essex and Foche, he apparently went by Sturrey as well, using the name of the manor near Canterbury granted him on 3 February 1538/9.[66] As for Dygon, both that name and

---

[63] I am grateful to Thomas Mathiesen for pointing out this reading of the inscription, which resolves one of the manuscript's major issues. In addition, with the removal of the dative element, it seems likely that the second name should read "Vuylborus" and not "Vuylborns," as a Latin version of "Wylbore" constructed in the same manner as "Dygonus" (which is quite clearly the reading of the first name, not "Dygouns"; see fig. 1c). Ronald Woodley reminds me, moreover, that the term "modo" can convey the sense of recent time—in this case indicating that the change from Dygon to Wylbore occurred not long before the writing of this inscription. Such an interpretation meshes remarkably well with the manuscript dating suggested on pp. 63–64 *infra*.

[64] **GB**-Llp, Register of Thomas Cranmer, f. 395^{v}.

[65] Francis Aidan Gasquet, *Henry VIII and the English Monasteries*, rev. ed. (London: G. Bell, 1906), 123, n. 2.

[66] *Letters and Papers* 14/1, no. 651/34: among the grants to Sir Edward Boughton (March 1539), "all lands, &c., which John Essex *alias* Sturrey, late abbot of the said late monastery [*sc.* St. Augustine's] held in Plumstede." For the grant of Sturrey to Essex, see *Letters and Papers* 14/1, no. 1355, Book 233, f. 141^{v}. The abbot had already been using this manor for many years by the time of the Dissolution, according to Twyne's account; see p. 21 *infra*.

Wylbore are common enough in the sixteenth-century documentation to indicate the presence of numerous families with these names throughout England. Stanley Boorman and Roger Bowers suggest that the composer may have taken the name Dygon on account of the patronage of the elder abbot John Dygon, with Wylbore being his family name.[67] The new reading of the inscription in **GB**-Ctc O.3.38 offers, in any case, a temporal element that, connected to the details of Dygon's biography, will have repercussions for the dating of the manuscript (see pp. 60–64 *infra*).

As John Wylbore, the musician lived for at least another nineteen years, although the popularity of the names Wylbore and Dygon adds considerable uncertainty to his identification in post-Dissolution documents. We know that he is not the same man as the John Wildbore who was a canon at Rochester in the 1540s, a Cambridge graduate who was buried in Rochester Cathedral in 1552 (several years before the last definite reference to Dygon/Wylbore).[68] Dygon's appointment as vicar of Preston in 1545 has been mentioned above. A John Wilbore was made vicar of St. Mary's Church, Minster (a parish in the gift of St. Augustine's, as noted by Boorman and Bowers[69]) on 7 February 1549/50. Both vicarages were resigned in 1557.[70] The name of John Wylbore also appears among several holders of properties in Canterbury granted to James Hales in September 1545.[71] The only candidate in burial records for identification with the composer is a "John Heaviside, *alias* Dygon, former monk" in 1566, listed in the Parish Register of St. Andrew in the Canterbury Cathedral Archives.[72]

Laying aside the uncertainties concerning Dygon's later biography, it is possible to find in the environment of St. Augustine's Monastery a suitable context for the prior's learned pursuits. The sole surviving catalogue of books owned by the abbey at an early period, compiled probably in the 1490s, demonstrates the breadth of written learning available to the monks in its ca. 1830 volumes (and even this is an incomplete list).[73] At least two

---

[67]Boorman, "Dygon, John," 7:816.

[68]Emden, *A Biographical Register*, 182.

[69]Boorman, "Dygon, John," 7:816.

[70]Noted in T. Shipdem Frampton, "St. Mary's Church, Minster, Isle of Thanet: List of Vicars," *Archaeologia Cantiana* 25 (1902): 104.

[71]*Letters and Papers* 20/2, no. 496.

[72]William Urry, *Christopher Marlowe and Canterbury* (London: Faber, 1988), 9 and 148, n. 44.

[73]The manuscript catalogue, preserved today at Trinity College, Dublin as MS. 360 (Bernard 285), is transcribed and discussed in M. R. James, *The Ancient Libraries of Can-*

manuscripts of the library (nos. 1115 and 1116) contained music tracts, their contents displaying a traditional outlook typical of music theory compilations preserved and created in fifteenth-century England.[74] The first of these contained a "Musica Johannis" without further specification, *Musica enchiriadis*, and one other unspecified *musica*; the second book included two tracts identified as *Musica guidonis* (one of these by "W. de Cicestria"), as well as a "Musica Augi" that is presumably the *De musica* of Augustine.[75] Both of these manuscripts could well have been several centuries old by Dygon's lifetime, although the transmission of venerable theoretical works and their use in university courses remained a reality throughout Europe into the sixteenth century.[76] Presumably Dygon encountered more treatises like these alongside the books of Boethius and Johannes de Muris when he studied music at Oxford. Moreover, if the notes in John Tucke's manuscript are at all representative of an Oxonian music education during these years, a grounding in elements of *musica practica* (including the proportions applied in mensural music) would have been a significant aspect of Dygon's studies; this assumption is supported likewise by the largely standardized requirement of composing a mass and antiphon for the B.Mus. or D.Mus. at Oxford.[77]

The support of Dygon's superiors at St. Augustine's must have played a significant role in encouraging his studies, as is suggested by various

---

terbury and Dover (Cambridge: Cambridge University Press, 1903), lvi–lxxx and 173–406. The dating of the book is in fact based on the appearance of the name John Dygon in a register at the front, without any indication of special rank. James suggests that this is the elder Dygon, who became abbot in 1497, but one must also bear in mind that from 1509 until 1521 there was only a single Dygon, of junior status, at St. Augustine's. The *terminus post quem* for the catalogue is set by the inclusion of a book dated 1491.

[74]James, *The Ancient Libraries*, 319. As far as I know, these volumes have not been identified with any surviving books; their second folio incipits are "ad aequalem" and "cura fit." For an overview of theory transmission in fifteenth-century England, see Dumitrescu, "Anglo-Continental Musical Relations," 1:183–203.

[75]The title *Musica guidonis* is generally applied now to a treatise transmitted in **GB**-Lbl Lansdowne 763 and **GB**-Ob Bodley 77 but thought to date from at least a century before its sources; see Cecily Sweeney, "John Wylde and the Musica Guidonis," *Musica disciplina* 29 (1977): 43–59. The St. Augustine's catalogue suggests, however, that this title was applied to a number of different works.

[76]See Nan Cooke Carpenter, *Music in the Medieval and Renaissance Universities* (Norman: University of Oklahoma Press, 1958). Even part of the English *Quatuor principalia* of the fourteenth century made its way into an early sixteenth-century Ghent manuscript alongside writings by Tinctoris and other authors, covering a span of several centuries; see Aluas, "The *Quatuor principalia musicae*," 35–36 and 189–97.

[77]Bray, "Music and the Quadrivium," 5–8.

sources. Along with the humanistically inclined superiors of Christchurch, Canterbury (for example, the scholar and diplomat William Selling[78]), the abbots of St. Augustine's came into contact with the political and intellectual leaders of the day on various occasions. When an imperial embassy came through Canterbury in 1507/8 to negotiate a marriage between Henry VII's daughter Mary and Prince Charles of Castile, the party designated to welcome the company included not only the mayor and aldermen of the city but also the prior of Christchurch and the abbot of St. Augustine's (at that point, the elder John Dygon).[79] The value placed on higher learning at St. Augustine's was expressed formally in the Customary, as noted by Harrison: "At St. Augustine's, Canterbury, a young monk who showed special ability might be given dispensation from his duties in the monastery and be sent to the university (*ad studium*), provided he knew by heart the Psalter, Hymnal and canticles, the *Commune Sanctorum*, the week-day antiphons and short responds, and the verses of the Antiphonal."[80] How many times Dygon took up this opportunity is difficult to gauge; apart from the Oxford B.Mus. in 1512, as mentioned above, we have evidence of studies at Paris and Leuven, and a bachelor's degree in theology. Such an array of university experiences could well seem too much to credit to one individual, but the single primary testimonial to Dygon's character does in fact portray a scholar of broad learning. Twyne's *De rebus albionicis*, mentioned earlier as the source for our knowledge of Dygon's continental travels, takes the form of a fictional conversation between Abbot Essex/Foche of St. Augustine's, Dygon, and Nicholas Wotton, concerning early British history. Set in the 1520s (shortly after Dygon and Wotton had returned to England with Vives) at Essex's manor of Sturrey, the book reveals the high esteem in which its author held these men on account of their morals and knowledge of history.[81] Twyne describes Dygon as "Prior integerrimus cænobij *Augustiniani*" (while noting that he was not yet prior at the time in which the book

---

[78]See Francis Aidan Gasquet, *The Eve of the Reformation* (London: Bell, 1900; reprint, Port Washington, NY: Kennikat Press, 1971), 26–28 and 30–33.

[79]*The solempnities. & triumphes doon & made at the spousellis and Mariage of the kyngis doughter the Ladye Marye to the Prynce of Castile Archeduke of Austrige* (London: Richarde Pynson, 1508; reprint in Roxburghe Club Publications, no. 23, London: Roxburghe Club, 1818).

[80]Frank Ll. Harrison, *Music in Medieval Britain* (London: Routledge and Paul, 1958), 39.

[81]"Ex multis verò quos ego egregiè ac praetèr caeteros colui dùm viuebant, cùm proptèr morum grauitatem summam, tùm rerum antiquarum cognitionem eximiam, fuerunt, si non nouisti, *Ioannes Vochius, & Ioannes Digonius*" (Twyne, *De rebus albionicis*, 4).

is set) and "summa vitae sanctitate senex florentissimus" (along with Essex). Wotton, noted as the youngest of the three (born ca. 1497), rose in later years to political importance as a diplomat, secretary of state, and dean of Canterbury and York, having obtained a doctorate in divinity as well as civil and canon law; he spent much of his career at various centers on the Continent.[82] According to Twyne, these three "viri clarissimi" met on numerous occasions to discuss matters of antiquity; perhaps these sessions followed the course adopted in Twyne's text, with Essex acting as leader of the discussion and offering learned discourses in response to the questions of Wotton and Dygon. The most laconic of Twyne's characters (apart from the author-narrator, who merely observes the conversation) is Dygon, whose interjections are rare. In an instance where Dygon quotes from the *Argonautica* of Valerius Flaccus, the other characters praise his learning in *literae prophanae*, noting the exceptional nature of this knowledge outside the bounds of *literae sacrae*. Dygon, for his part, replies with modesty.[83]

As mentioned above, the sole source of compositions by Dygon outside **GB**-Ctc O.3.38 is Baldwin's book from near the end of the sixteenth century (**GB**-Lbl R.M. 24.d.2, ff. 165^{v}–166^{r}). These works are short three-voice passages, which are probably sections extracted from longer pieces for larger forces. Two of the sections, *Ad lapidis posicionem* and *quod enim vivit deo* use texts from the Easter processional antiphon *Christus resurgens* and its verse *Dicant nunc judei*, with identical scoring (C4-C4-F4); the other three sections set the texts *Rex benedicte*, *ut tergant miseras*, and *atque colant* from the Lenten antiphon *O rex gloriose* in a higher cleffing (C3-C3-C4). In both cases, quotation of the plainchant antiphons at section openings (usually in the lowest voice) confirms the association of these short sections with the longer antiphons.[84] The various sections in total thus make up parts of two separate works, and it is in this form that they are edited in the Appendix to the present volume. The writing in these compositions belongs stylistically to the first decades of the sixteenth century, mixing a rhythmically involved and syncopated manner with a combination of structural and incidental imitation; for examples of generally similar writing, compare

---

[82]Leslie Stephen and Sidney Lee, eds., *Dictionary of National Biography ... from the Earliest Times to 1900*, 22 vols. (London: Oxford University Press, 1949–50), 21:972–76.

[83]Twyne, *De rebus albionicis*, 19–21.

[84]*Antiphonale Sarisburiense*, ed. Walter Howard Frere (London: Plainsong and Mediaeval Music Society, 1901–26), 190–91 and 241–42.

the sections for reduced scorings in works such as Ashwell's *Missa Jhesu criste*.[85]

It is perhaps striking that these examples of Dygon's compositional style show such little interest in proportional writing (especially considering that Baldwin had included an entire section of proportionally involved compositions earlier in the manuscript), but the one instance of proportional usage confirms one of the idiosyncratic practices demonstrated in Dygon's treatises. In m. 82 of *Rex benedicte*, the brief overlap of *tripla* in the top voice with *quadrupla* in the second voice produces a semibrevis's worth of *sesquitertia* in the 3:4 relationship between the parts, which is precisely one of the forms of proportional writing Dygon added to Gaffurius's text in his own version.[86] For the question of Dygon's identity, this passage helps to confirm that the composer of the works in Baldwin's book, noted explicitly as the prior of St. Augustine's, is the same as the redactor of the treatises in **GB**-Ctc O.3.38 (and presumably the holder of the Oxford B.Mus. as well).

Taken as a whole, the scattered elements of Dygon's biography point to a scholar who was well placed to create the set of theoretical writings found in the Cambridge manuscript. As a young monk who perhaps owed his place at St. Augustine's in the early years of the sixteenth century to the abbot of the same name, Dygon would have had access to a wealth of learning in the monastery's library. That he took advantage of the opportunity is suggested by his supplication for the B.Mus. at the University of Oxford in 1512, which is the only documentary evidence, outside the music and theory sources, of the monk's musical skills. In the early 1520s, a period of study at the northern centers of learning on the Continent offered the musician a chance to encounter texts, ideas, and teachers unavailable to him in Canterbury and Oxford; whether this sojourn was made for the purpose of musical studies or for one of Dygon's various other academic interests is impossible to say. It seems certain that the composer's learning in different fields was one of the qualities that ingratiated him with Abbot Essex, leading to his eventual promotion to the status of prior of the abbey. There is no indication that Dygon's musical activities were limited to any one period, and the composition of the treatises could have taken place at any time from the composer's Oxford years to the Dissolution or even beyond (although the compositional and notational styles would be considerably dated by the

[85]Edited in *Early Tudor Masses: II*, ed. John Bergsagel, Early English Church Music, vol. 16 (London: Stainer and Bell, 1976), 1–72. This general dating of the Dygon works is strengthened by the compositions' placement in the manuscript, on the opening before a *Quam pulcra es* ascribed to Henry VIII in a generally retrospective section of the book.

[86]See pp. 43–44 *infra*.

later years of the musician's life; see below). The documentary evidence does not allow for the supposition that the John Dygon of St. Augustine's was not the same man as the composer and theorist: the appearance of the names Dygon and Wylbore together in **GB**-Ctc O.3.38, together with the identification in Baldwin's book of Dygon as prior of St. Augustine's, in fact, connects all of the music surviving under this name to the monk. The fortunate survival of the Cambridge manuscript, then, offers a window onto the musical activities of a man of university and monastic circles, a learned scholar who—like so many university thinkers and music theorists of the period—extended his academic interests far beyond a single discipline.

Design and Content of the Treatises

On the surface, **GB**-Ctc O.3.38 offers few clues to the purposes behind its compilation and the principles guiding its structure. The manuscript lacks any sort of listing of its contents, along with any introductory and closing texts to offer a context for its instructional material.[87] Equally significant is the absence of any acknowledgement of the major source for the book's text, Book IV of Gaffurius's *Practica musice*. The only immediately apparent structures on a large scale are the division into two texts or treatises (separated by a blank page, with the ascription to Dygon ending the first of these) and the ordering of each treatise by proportional *genus* (made apparent by the centered headings preceding the material covering each *genus*). That the latter structure is adopted wholesale from Gaffurius's treatise is obscured slightly by Dygon's removal of chapter numbers, but this is by no means a major modification in comparison to some of the other changes in Dygon's version of the text.

A detailed examination of each of the two texts in the manuscript follows, in which each text is viewed as a separate treatise in its own right. This division is suggested by the presentation of the works in the source, where the authorial "Quod"-formula acts as an *explicit* to the first text, as confirmed by the following blank space. Furthermore, the return at the start of the second text to the first proportion (*dupla*) and the parallel course of the two texts—they follow the same ordering of proportions—reveal that the second section is a reworking of the first, created for the demonstration of a different system of proportional notation. The two items, then, are related in an intimate manner, and the stylistic similarities extend to the reuse of text from the first treatise (and originally from Gaffurius's book) in the second. If we can deduce that these are the work of the same author-

[87]For a discussion of the manuscript's physical attributes and structure, see "The Manuscript" *infra*.

editor and were probably intended to be read together for greatest utility, the texts nevertheless invite separate treatment, and the interest aroused by each is of a different nature.

Treatise 1: The Adaptation of Gaffurius

Of the two treatises, the first is the more extended, as well as the one that draws the most from the *Practica musice.* As mentioned above, the "Quod" formula is not always intended to represent original authorship (itself a much more fluid concept in the sixteenth century than in modern times), and the present case involves a particular style of selection and reworking from Gaffurius's text. In table 1 (on the following pages), the elements included in the books of Gaffurius and Dygon are compared side-by-side, illustrating the complex and varied nature of the borrowings and additions present in the Cambridge manuscript.

If it seems that the fourth book of the *Practica musice* is mostly a repetitive enumeration of proportions illustrated by musical examples, the version by Dygon acts even more explicitly as a work of pure reference. Dygon skips Gaffurius's careful introduction, with its technical definition of proportion and references to ancient authorities, and starts directly at the "practical" section of the book, beginning with the *genus multiplex* and examples of its species. Of the fifteen chapters in Book IV of the *Practica musice*, material from only five of these forms the basis for the text in **GB-Ctc** O.3.38; these are, however, from the core chapters that form the bulk of Gaffurius's discussion. These chapters, furthermore, contain the majority of the practical examples with which the Italian theorist demonstrates his proportions, and Dygon's replacement of most of these examples with fresh compositions produces a significant body of original material in the English manuscript. Not a single page of Dygon's copy lacks a musical example, and most pages contain at least two; the English musician additionally managed to include numerous practical demonstrations of a type of proportional writing not found in the Italian source (to be discussed below). With regard to the textual material, Dygon's omission of various digressions in which Gaffurius considers the technicalities of contemporaneous notational practice (for example, his discussion of how to notate *sesquialtera* properly) is offset by the insertion of comments that appear to relate the English monk's own practical concerns.

Table 1: Comparison of Gaffurius, *Practica musice* (1496), Book IV, with the first Dygon treatise (**GB**-Ctc O.3.38, ff. 1^r–12^r)

Cap.	Gaffurius only	Gaffurius and Dygon[a]	Dygon only
1	Definition of proportion		
2	Description of *genera* of proportions		
3		*Genus multiplex* **definition**	
	cancellation of *dupla* through *subdupla* indicating *dupla* with a canon mensuration signs with numerals	***dupla***	note on possible rhythmic levels for *dupla* (minima, semibrevis, rarely brevis)
	cancellation of *multiplex* proportions through corresponding *submultiplex* proportions loss of value of larger number in *quintupla* and other proportions	*tripla / quadrupla / quintupla / sextupla / septupla / octupla*	*inductiones* for *sextupla* confusion of *sextupla* and *tripla* *sextupla* at the level of the minima too quick for performance
	nonupla / decupla		
4	*Genus submultiplex*		
5		*Genus superparticulare* **definition**	
	slightly extended definition		
	common ways (correct and incorrect) of notating *sesquialtera*	*sesquialtera*	
	use of Ɔ to show *sesquitertia* cancellation of *superparticulare* proportions through corresponding *subsuperparticulare* proportions	*sesquitertia / sesquiquarta / sesquiquinta / sesquisexta / sesquiseptima / sesquioctava*	3-voice examples producing *superparticulare* proportions through use of simultaneous *multiplex* proportions phrase questioning whether anyone can sing *septupla* correctly
	sesquinona		
6	*Genus subsuperparticulare*		

Cap.	Gaffurius only	Gaffurius and Dygon[a]	Dygon only
7	extended definition	*Genus superpartiens* **definition**	
	cancellation of *superpartiens* proportions through corresponding *subsuperpartiens* proportions	***superbipartiens tertias*** / *superbipartiens quintas* / *superbipartiens septimas* / *supertripartiens quartas* / *supertripartiens quintas* / *supertripartiens septimas* / *superquatripartiens quintas* / *superquatripartiens septimas* / *superquatripartiens nonas* / *superquincupartiens sextas* / *superquincupartiens septimas* / *supersexcupartiens septimas*	3-voice examples producing *superpartiens* proportions through use of simultaneous *multiplex* or *multiplex superpartiens* proportions
8	*Genus subsuperpartiens*		
9		*Genus multiplex superparticulare* **definition**	
	cancellation of *multiplex superparticulare* proportions through corresponding *submultiplex superparticulare* proportions	*dupla sesquialtera* / *dupla sesquitertia* / *dupla sesquiquarta* / *dupla sesquiquinta* / *tripla sesquialtera* / *tripla sesquitertia* / *tripla sesquiquarta* / *quadrupla sesquialtera* / *quadrupla sesquitertia* / *quadrupla sesquiquarta* / *quintupla sesquialtera* / *quintupla sesquitertia* / *quintupla sesquiquarta*	*tripla* and *sesquialtera* as *inductiones* for *quadrupla sesquialtera*
10	*Genus submultiplex superparticulare*		

Cap.	Gaffurius only	Gaffurius and Dygon[a]	Dygon only
11	slightly extended definition	*Genus multiplex superpartiens* **definition** *dupla superbipartiens tertias / dupla superbipartiens quintas / dupla supertripartiens quartas / dupla supertripartiens quintas / tripla superbipartiens tertias / tripla superbipartiens quintas / tripla supertripartiens quartas / tripla supertripartiens quintas / quadrupla superbipartiens tertias / quadrupla superbipartiens quintas / quadrupla supertripartiens quartas*	"Qd' Joannes Dygonus M° Vuylborus."
12	*Genus submultiplex superpartiens*		
13	Successive application of proportions		
14	Proportions of consonances		
15	Producing the *genus multiplex* by combining *multiplex* and *superparticulare* Conclusion of *Practica musice*		

[a]**Bold text** indicates near-exact correspondence; other items are close paraphrase.

It will be useful here to have a brief overview of the proportional theory underlying the fourth book of the *Practica musice* as well as Dygon's treatises. The basic definition of a proportion as used in these works is simply a ratio—or comparative relation of two numbers. A fundamental element of western music theory since Boethius's transmission of Greek theoretical principles, the study of proportions lay at the root of medieval speculation concerning musical consonance and the construction of a pitch space. This traditional aspect of music theory, however, was joined in the fourteenth and fifteenth centuries by newer applications of proportions in the sphere of *musica practica*, as noted above. By employing numerical proportions to affect musical rhythm at a local level, musicians exposed their solidifying system of rhythmic notation to the possibilities available in the infinite series of ratios. The generalization of proportional rhythmic practice that accompanied the use of Hindu-Arabic numerals created a clearer and more extensible system of proportional notation than is possible through the use of mensuration signs alone. The *Practica musice* was among the first writings to draw out this proportion system to a logical extent beyond the practical limits of contemporaneous style and to explore the subject with a comprehensive and systematic treatment.

The plan Gaffurius adopted in his book, once past the introductory material, follows a straightforward progression through the ten proportional *genera*, from simplest to most complex: *multiplex*, *submultiplex*, *superparticulare*, *subsuperparticulare*, *superpartiens*, *subsuperpartiens*, *multiplex superparticulare*, *submultiplex superparticulare*, *multiplex superpartiens*, and *submultiplex superpartiens*. Within each *genus*, a series of proportions is considered, in rising numerical order. The *genus multiplex* contains all proportions in which the first (larger) number is a multiple of the second; for example, *dupla* (2:1), *tripla* (3:1), and *quadrupla* (4:1). The *genus submultiplex* covers a corresponding set of proportions in which the second number is a multiple of the first, as in *subdupla* (1:2). In the proportions of the *genus superparticulare* and the *genus subsuperparticulare*, the larger number is greater than the smaller number by an amount that is a factor of the smaller number (this factor is known as an "aliquot" part); examples include *sesquialtera* (3:2), *sesquitertia* (4:3), *sesquiquarta* (5:4), and the corresponding *subsesquialtera* (2:3), *subsesquitertia* (3:4), and *subsesquiquarta* (4:5).

The relation of the numbers in the proportions of the *genus superpartiens* and the *genus subsuperpartiens* is such that the larger number is greater than the smaller number by an amount that is not a factor of the smaller number but is still less than the smaller number (this amount is called an "aliquant" part); these include, for example, *superbipartiens tertias* (5:3), *superbipartiens quintas* (7:5), *supertripartiens quartas* (7:4), and the corresponding *subsuperbipartiens tertias* (3:5), *subsuperbipartiens quintas* (5:7), and *subsupertripartiens quartas* (4:7). The naming convention for proportions in the *genus superpartiens* and the *genus subsuperpartiens* involves two numerical elements that together describe the size of the aliquant part. In the form "Super[A]partiens [B]" element B corresponds to an aliquot division of the smaller number in the proportion, while element A corresponds to the number of such aliquot parts that go into the aliquant part, that is, the difference between the two numbers in the proportion. In "Super**tri**partiens **quartas**," then, the smaller number is divided by four and the result is multiplied by three to yield the difference between the numbers in the proportion, as in 14:8 or 7:4. A simpler way to express this example is to state that in *supertripartiens quartas* the larger number is greater than the smaller number by ¾ of the smaller number (see table 2 *infra* for a generalized formula with further examples).

The remaining *genera* arise from a combination of the *genus multiplex* and the *genus submultiplex* with the *genus superparticulare* and the *genus superpartiens*. In the proportions of the *genus multiplex superparticulare* and the *genus submultiplex superparticulare*, the smaller number is multiplied by a certain amount and added to one of its factors to yield the larger number; for example, *dupla sesquialtera* (5:2), *dupla sesquitertia* (7:3), *tripla sesquiquinta* (16:5), and the corresponding *subdupla sesquialtera* (2:5), *subdupla sesquitertia* (3:7), and *subtripla sesquiquinta* (5:16). Finally, the *genus multiplex superpartiens* and the *genus submultiplex superpartiens* include proportions in which the smaller number is multiplied by a certain amount and added to one of its aliquant parts to yield the larger number; examples of these are *dupla superbipartiens tertias* (8:3), *dupla superquatripartiens quintas* (14:5), *tripla supertripartiens quintas* (18:5), and the corresponding *subdupla superbipartiens tertias* (3:8), *subdupla superquatripartiens quintas* (5:14), and *subtripla supertripartiens quintas* (5:18).

Together the ten *genera* describe every possible relationship of two unequal positive integers. As a further element of descriptive nomenclature, those *genera* in which the first number is greater than the second (*multiplex, superparticulare, superpartiens, multiplex superparticulare, multiplex superpartiens*) are known as the *genera* of greater inequality ("genera maioris inequalitatis"), while those *genera* in which the first number is less than the second (*submultiplex, subsuperparticulare, subsuperpartiens, submultiplex superparticulare, submultiplex superpartiens*) are known as the *genera* of lesser inequality ("genera minoris inequalitatis"). In table 2, the relationship covered by each *genus* is expressed as an algebraic ratio, describing ratios only in their lowest terms for simplicity (reducing 6:8 to 3:4, for example; non-reduced forms can be derived by multiplying each side of each ratio by the same positive integer).

Table 2: Proportional *genera*

Name of *genus*	**Ratio (in lowest terms)**	**Examples**
Multiplex	xy : x (where y≥1)	2:1 (*dupla*) 3:1 (*tripla*) 6:2 (*tripla*)
Submultiplex	x : xy (where y≥1)	1:2 (*subdupla*) 1:3 (*subtripla*) 2:6 (*subtripla*)
Superparticulare	x+1 : x	3:2 (*sesquialtera*) 4:3 (*sesquitertia*) 8:6 (*sesquitertia*)
Subsuperparticulare	x : x+1	2:3 (*subsesquialtera*) 3:4 (*subsesquitertia*) 6:8 (*subsesquitertia*)
Superpartiens	x+y : x (where x>y>1, y is not a factor of x)	5:3 (*superbipartiens tertias*) 7:4 (*supertripartiens quartas*) 14:8 (*supertripartiens quartas*)
Subsuperpartiens	x : x+y (where x>y>1, y is not a factor of x)	3:5 (*subsuperbipartiens tertias*) 4:7 (*subsupertripartiens quartas*) 8:14 (*subsupertripartiens quartas*)
Multiplex superparticulare	yx+1 : x (where y>1)	5:2 (*dupla sesquialtera*) 7:2 (*tripla sesquialtera*) 14:4 (*tripla sesquialtera*)
Submultiplex superparticulare	x : yx+1 (where y>1)	2:5 (*subdupla sesquialtera*) 2:7 (*subtripla sesquialtera*) 4:14 (*subtripla sesqui-altera*)
Multiplex superpartiens	yx+z : x (where x>z>1 and y>1)	8:3 (*dupla superbipartiens tertias*) 15:4 (*tripla supertripar-tiens quartas*) 30:8 (*tripla supertripar-tiens quartas*)
Submultiplex superpartiens	x : yx+z (where x>z>1 and y>1)	3:8 (*subdupla superbipar-tiens tertias*) 4:15 (*subtripla supertri-partiens quartas*) 8:30 (*subtripla supertri-partiens quartas*)

The system described above is both a consistent and a regular one, and in the ordering of its *genera* gives the body of Gaffurius's discussion its form.

For the version transmitted by Dygon, however, a significant modification is the consistent omission of all *genera* of lesser inequality (see table 1 above). While on first inspection a seemingly minor change, since these *genera* simply mirror the *genera* of greater inequality, the absence of this set in the Cambridge manuscript has conceptual and notational repercussions. The examples in this portion of the *Practica musice* normally begin a proportional section with two arabic numerals representing a proportion of greater inequality (for example, *tripla*, 3:1), causing diminution in one voice (the Cantus). To return to normal note values, one of two methods is employed: either the proportion is cancelled through the corresponding proportion of lesser inequality (in the case of *tripla* cited above, this would be *subtripla*, 1:3), again represented with Hindu-Arabic numerals, or a new mensuration sign appears. In the first case, each time a new proportion is used, it is related solely to the music preceding it in that voice, creating a series of cumulative rhythmic transformations. Dygon, however, in skipping the proportions of lesser inequality, does not have this option in his examples. As a result, there are only cases of diminution and not augmentation in the English manuscript. Consequently, in order to use a section of proportional writing that finishes before the end of an example, Dygon must use a mensuration sign to return one voice to equality with the other (as in the sequence O 2:1 O or C 3:2 C). This method and the one found in Gaffurius's examples differ in that each proportion in Dygon's Discantus is related conceptually to the simultaneous music of the Tenor rather than to the preceding music in the Discantus; there is no cumulative effect of proportions in one voice. A clear demonstration of this point can be found in the example of *sextupla* on f. 2^{r} (pp. 76–77 *infra*), where 3:2 is immediately followed by 6:1, and 3:1 is immediately followed by 12:2.[88] In contrapuntal terms, the *sextupla* sections (6:1 and 12:2) must be six times faster than the music at the start of the example; had the proportions been cumulative, however, the first *sextupla* section would have to be six times faster than the preceding 3:2 section (i.e., nine times faster than the music at the start) and the second *sextupla* section would have to be six times faster than the preceding 3:1 section (i.e., eighteen times faster than the music at the start).

Less significant omissions in Dygon's version of the text include several proportions in the *genus multiplex* and the *genus superparticulare*: where Gaffurius illustrates cases from *dupla* (2:1) to *decupla* (10:1) and *sesquialtera* (3:2) to *sesquinona* (10:9), Dygon cuts off after *octupla* (8:1) and *sesquioctava* (9:8). The English writer retains all of the proportions in the

---

[88]These are examples of *inductiones*; see pp. 9–10 *supra* and pp. 34–36 *infra*.

genus superpartiens, the *genus multiplex superparticulare*, and the *genus multiplex superpartiens*. In the definitions of *genera* that open each section of the treatise (corresponding to chapters in the *Practica musice*), the Cambridge manuscript largely transmits Gaffurius's text verbatim, with some consistent differences of orthography (such as the removal of Gaffurius's classicizing diphthongs). Dygon does, however, apply some degree of regularization to the definitions of the *genus superparticulare*, the *genus superpartiens*, and the *genus multiplex superpartiens*. The standard format employed in the English manuscript includes a basic mathematical description of each *genus*, followed by a listing of proportions within the *genus*, before the text moves on to the treatment of individual proportions. For the *genus superparticulare* and the *genus multiplex superpartiens*, adherence to this format entails a simple removal of some descriptive text following the listing of proportions; it is perhaps noteworthy that the extra text ommitted in the *genus superparticulare* (chapter 5) includes an explicit reference to Gaffurius's (then forthcoming) *De harmonia musicorum instrumentorum opus*.[89] In the *genus superpartiens*, on the other hand, Gaffurius offers a significantly more thorough introduction than Dygon, proceeding through several *species* within the *genus* in order (*superbipartiens*, *supertripartiens*, and *superquatripartiens*) and touching upon certain mathematical properties of the same. Dygon's version of the definition is quite spare in comparison, presenting only the essential attributes of the *genus*.

To a large extent, then, the English musician's approach to editing the Italian treatise centers on fitting the text into a regular and schematic structure. Issues of practical performance account for a good deal of the deviations from such a format in Gaffurius's discussion; the absence of these sections in **GB**-Ctc O.3.38 may result not only from a regularizing impulse but also from a lack of relevance for English theory. The consideration of mensuration signs combined with numerals in common use, concluding Gaffurius's treatment of *dupla*, touches on a subject that was a concern of continental theorists; but these signs made little headway into contemporaneous English sources. Likewise, the considerable trouble caused by the interpretation of *sesquialtera* induced Gaffurius to include an extended discussion of its notation, which is left out of the Cambridge treatise. In practical contexts, certain English scribes may have been more conscientious than their continental counterparts, for example in the use of both numerals to show *sesquialtera* in **GB**-WRec 178 (The Eton Choirbook). In the case of *sesquitertia*, Gaffu-

[89] Franchinus Gaffurius, *De harmonia musicorum instrumentorum opus* (Milan: Gotardus Pontanus, 1518; reprint, New York: Broude Bros., 1979); idem, *Practica musice*, sig. ffviij^{v}.

rius includes a passage indicating writers who have criticized the practice of using Ↄ to show the proportion; Dygon's second treatise in fact treats this sign as the only acceptable means of denoting *sesquitertia*.[90]

The Cambridge text, however, is not lacking in its own brief digressions, and we encounter in these passages the practical interests of the English writer. As mentioned above, Dygon's passages on *inductiones*, inserted after the example of *sextupla* (f. 2^{r}, pp. 76–77 *infra*) and in the description of *quadrupla sesquialtera* (f. 8^{v}, pp. 116–17 *infra*), provide corroboration for statements describing this practice in English writings from the early and late years of the century (Pace in 1518 and Morley in 1597).[91] The idea of using common proportions to lead into larger or more complex proportions works on a principle of succession. For a relatively simple proportion such as *sextupla*, the process might seem to introduce needless complexity, as Morley suggested: it is probably just as easy for the performer to apply *sextupla* directly as it is to use *sesquialtera* or *tripla* first, thereafter applying another level of *quadrupla* or *dupla* (respectively) to yield *sextupla*.

Table 3: *Inductiones* in examples of **GB**-Ctc O.3.38

F.	Proportion demonstrated	Sequence of proportions
2^{r}	*Sextupla*	3:2 → 6:1
		3:1 → 12:2
4^{r}	*Sesquisexta*	3:2 → 6:1
4^{v}	*Sesquioctava*	3:2 → 9:2
6^{r}	*Superquatripartiens quintas*	3:2 → 9:2
8^{v}	*Quadrupla sesquialtera*	3:1 → 3:2 → 9:2
17^{v}	*Quadrupla sesquialtera*	3:2 (minima) → 3:2 (semibrevis) → O:C [9:2]
		3:1 → ⊙:C [9:2]

The utility of the practice is more obvious, however, in the various examples where Dygon leads into *quadrupla sesquialtera* (9:2) with these same two *inductiones*, *tripla* and *sesquialtera* (see table 3, which lists all uses of *inductiones* in the examples of the manuscript).[92] A performer who is already in *sesquialtera* need only apply a further level of *tripla* to yield

[90] See pp. 144–45 *infra*.

[91] See pp. 9–10 *supra*.

[92] *Sesquialtera* appears as an *inductio* of *quadrupla sesquialtera* several times before Dygon makes the relationship explicit on f. 8^{v}: "Si hanc proportionem [*sc.* quadruplam-sesqualteram] recte commensurare volueris, accipias velim has duas proportiones id est triplam et sesqualteram pro inductione" (pp. 116–17 *infra*).

quadrupla sesquialtera (i.e., 3:2 × 3:1 = 9:2). *Tripla* as an *inductio* of *quadrupla sesquialtera*, on the other hand, appears as a special case. On f. 8v, it is in fact used to lead into *sesquialtera*, which then leads to *quadrupla sesquialtera* (thus, the performer goes through the simple successive application of *tripla*, *subdupla*, then *tripla* again: 3:1 × 1:2 × 3:1 = 9:2). The case of *tripla* leading directly into *quadrupla sesquialtera* on f. 17v involves a situation where the *tripla* lasts for a single semibrevis, followed by a *quadrupla sesquialtera* segment that is designated explicitly in the text as occurring at the level of the minima:

For the performer looking for a simple path leading to *quadrupla sesquialtera*, the application of *sesquialtera* after only a single semibrevis's worth of *tripla* would be a complex enough operation to negate any value of using the *inductio*. The rhythmic character of the example at this point, however, is designed specifically to aid the transition. The switch between *tripla* and *quadrupla sesquialtera* is indeed a case of *sesquialtera*, but with the accompanying shift from repeated semibreves to repeated minimae, what the performer experiences is a tripling of the rhythmic pace. The sequence of proportions leading to *quadrupla sesquialtera* in this example could have been notated equally well as a double application of *tripla* at the level of the semibrevis, which is undoubtedly the easiest way to conceive of it in performance:

It is in fact a similar situation that occurs in Morley's treatise, when *sesquialtera* is used in an example as an *inductio* to *quadrupla sesquialtera*, a simple tripling of the rhythmic pace. Although Morley, as noted above, had criticized the use of *inductiones* earlier in his book, here he was content to offer both a use and an explanation: "every Proportion whole is called the Induction to that which it maketh being broken, as Tripla being broken in the More Prolation will make Nonupla, and so is Tripla the Induction to Nonupla; or in the Less Prolation will make Sextupla, and so is the Induction to Sextupla. But let this suffice."[93] The exact arithmetic details of the progression need not have been a great concern to the performer. Rather, the successful operation of the system of *inductiones* depends upon the use of

[93] Morley, *A Plain and Easy Introduction* (ed. Harman), 172.

rhythmic shifts at transition points that are sufficiently common for performing musicians to have internalized them at an early stage of experience.

The mention of *inductiones* in connection with *sextupla* appears to have led Dygon into a brief digression on the notation and performance of *sextupla*:

Huic vero proportioni sextuple due, ut vides, inductiones sunt. prima sesqualtera. secunda tripla. quibus facile et vere hanc proportionem sextuplam mensurare queas. Multi vero et, ut dicam, indocti proportionem triplam pro sextupla componunt. sex enim minimas ad unam semibrevem imponunt. quod est tripla. Si sex minimas ad unam minimam. aut sex semibreves ad unam semibrevem componerent tunc proportionem sextuplam viderent. Set hec proportio sextupla ob celeritate nec facile digitis nec labiis per minimam exprimi potest. Semper igitur sextuplam, ut hic proponitur. per semibrevem componere solemus.[94]

However, this proportion *sextupla* has two *inductiones*, as you see. The first is *sesquialtera*, and the second is *tripla*. With these *inductiones* you can measure this proportion *sextupla* easily and truly. Many, however (and I would say, unlearned), compose in the proportion *tripla* in place of *sextupla*; for they set six minimae against one semibrevis, which is *tripla*. If they were to compose six minimae to one minima, or six semibreves to one semibrevis, then they would see the proportion *sextupla*. But on account of its swiftness, this proportion *sextupla* cannot be executed easily at the level of the minima, neither by fingers nor by lips; therefore we are accustomed always to compose the proportion *sextupla* at the level of the semibrevis, as is proposed here.

Confusion between *sextupla* and *tripla* may well have been an issue for beginning performers but does not seem to be a problem in the surviving sources. A case of this nature is perhaps represented by an example in the theory section of **GB**-Cmc Pepys 1236, where a demonstration of *sesquialtera* (with the word written on the example) is accompanied by the numeral 6 in the proportional voice (f. 108^{r}).[95] Finally, Dygon warns his readers that *sextupla* is not to be used except at the level of the semibrevis because it would otherwise be too quick to perform in minimae. As Dart

---

[94] F. 2^{r}, pp. 76–77 *infra*.

[95] The symbol could be explained as an error for a mensuration sign (Ͼ), but the dots on either side of the symbol suggest that to the scribe of the manuscript it was a numeral; the form of the numeral 6 in the list of Hindu-Arabic numerals on the preceding page (f. 107^{v}) corresponds exactly to that of the symbol in the example.

noticed, the phrase "nec ... digitis nec labiis" suggests the applicability of this proportional theory to both vocal and instrumental performance.[96]

This concern for performance lies behind occasional comments elsewhere in the manuscript, but the author seems well aware that many of his examples pass beyond the realm of practicality. An offhand remark questioning whether anyone can perform *septupla* correctly (f. 4^{r}, pp. 88–89 *infra*) is matched by the treatment of this proportion in Dygon's second treatise, where the unique absence of an example is explained with the comment "Septupla raro aut nunquam in usu est" (f. 14^{v}, pp. 142–43 *infra*). Several other proportions are singled out as not occurring in practice: *quintupla sesquitertia* (f. 9^{r}, pp. 118–19 *infra*), as well as all superparticular proportions greater than *sesquitertia* (in Treatise 2, f. 15^{r}, pp. 146–47 *infra*). The matter of which rhythmic levels are suitable for certain proportions appears at various points in the manuscript: *dupla* can be used at the level of the minima, semibrevis, and brevis, but the last of these only rarely (f. 1^{r}, pp. 70–71 *infra*), while all multiple proportions between *quintupla* and *octupla* are allowed only at the level of the semibrevis (f. 2^{r}, pp. 74–79 *infra*; Treatise 2, f. 14^{r-v}, pp. 140–43 *infra*).

For the close of the first treatise, the Cambridge manuscript again follows the formula of leaving out material extraneous to its purpose. The concluding chapters (13–15) of Gaffurius's compendium deal with specific subjects excluded in Dygon's proportion theory: the successive and cumulative application of proportions (which we have seen is not operative in Dygon's examples[97]); a brief discussion of combining the proportions that form consonances (a topic traditionally the domain of *musica theorica*); and the production of *multiplex* proportions through the successive application of the *genus multiplex* and the *genus superparticulare* (again relying on the cumulative proportional effect not recognized in the Cambridge book). The final conclusion of the entire *Practica musice*, of course, is not present in **GB**-Ctc O.3.38; Dygon (or the scribe) is content with the simple "Quod Joannes Dygonus Modo Vuylborus" following his final example, in place of any concluding remarks.

Undeniably, in assembling the first of the two treatises, Dygon drew directly on his Italian source for content—but the more important and more frequent adoption was of form and formula. The limited amount of direct quotation in the Cambridge manuscript is contained largely in the openings of sections in the form of initial definitions. For the treatment of individual

---

[96] Dart, "Origines et sources," 82.

[97] See p. 32 *supra.*

proportions in order, the *Practica musice* followed a standard format, and Dygon was able to employ this structure without following Gaffurius's text exactly for each proportion. The imitation of Gaffurius's ordering and approach is in fact one of the main links to the second treatise in **GB**-Ctc O.3.38, which takes the transformation of the original material one step further. Before considering the particularities of the second section of the manuscript, however, it will be useful to have an overview of the musical examples, which act as a further link between the two treatises in form and style.

Musical Examples in the Manuscript

Of the various departures from the Italian source treatise, the most significant body of new material in **GB**-Ctc O.3.38 is the large collection of newly composed examples that replaces and augments the set created by Gaffurius. Of the 81 (or 82) examples in the manuscript,[98] only two were copied from the *Practica musice*, and even these received modifications (see below). The examples are consistent in their general stylistic and notational features, suggesting the work of a single composer who clearly came from an English tradition. The only mensurations encountered are O and C,[99] and black void is the base color of the notation. The vast majority of proportional sections employ red coloration (usually full), with four instances of black void and two instances of black full (see table 4 *infra*); thanks to these exceptions, we find in the Cambridge manuscript exactly the four colors of music described in William Cornysh's allegorical poem known commonly as *A treatise bitwene Trowth and enformacion* (1504): "In musyke I have lernyde iiij colors as thys / blake full blake uoyde & in lyke wyse rede."[100] The English double-looped form of the round ♭ (customarily reserved for when the symbol lies on a staff line) occurs frequently but inconsistently. A related feature that resonates with English practice is the appearance of square ♮ (or *diesis*) and round ♭ signs in ♭-*fa*-♮-*mi* when they are technically superfluous; each of the six square ♮ signs marked in the first two examples

[98]The demonstration of *sesquitertia* on f. 3[r] is split into two short sections divided by a vertical line, a treatment that is unique in the manuscript; these sections can be considered to comprise one or two examples.

[99]Other signs such as Φ appear in the second treatise but do not have the force of mensuration signs; see pp. 48–52 *infra*.

[100]**GB**-Lbl Harley 43, f. 89[v]. On the readings of this source, possibly the earliest for Cornysh's poem, see Dumitrescu, "Anglo-Continental Musical Relations," 1:218–23 and 2:64–67. Red and black are also the only colors William Bathe had encountered in his examinations of older manuscripts and treatises (*A Briefe Introduction*, sig. Bv[r]).

of the book illustrates this habit (these examples demonstrate as well how many more square ♮ signs appear in the Cambridge book than in contemporaneous continental sources).[101] In certain melodic and contrapuntal details, Dygon's examples often employ forms more in favor in England than on the Continent. A case in point is provided by the modifications Dygon made to several cadences in the two examples copied from the *Practica musice*, illustrated in example 1 (the entire examples are transcribed in example 2 *infra*).

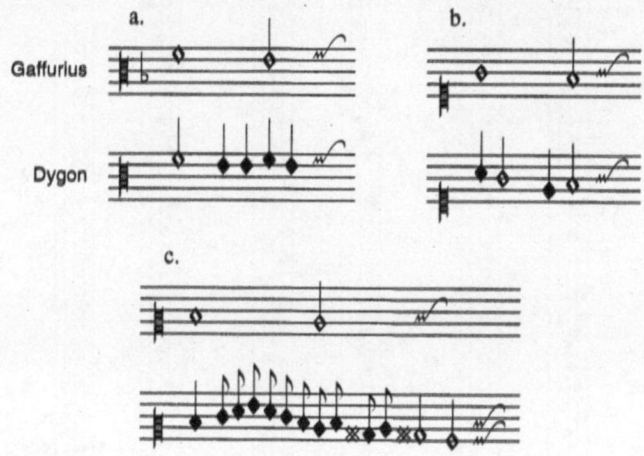

Example 1: Cadences in *Practica musice* examples as transmitted in **GB**-Ctc O.3.38, f. 6^r

Gaffurius was following perfectly normal practice in using the simple suspension form of the "cantizans" cadence: by the ending years of the fifteenth century, this was far and away the most frequently employed form in continental sources. English manuscripts of the later fifteenth and early sixteenth century, however, endow this figure with much less prominence, eschewing it in favor of forms that are both more ornamental and tend to avoid the use of suspension. The level of modification is at an extreme in example 1c, with its intricate flourish in fusae. Dygon goes so far as to change the underlying counterpoint to avoid a standard directed progression, dropping to a 6th instead of making the expected expansion to the octave (another manoeuver that has a bearing on the issue of distinctions between English and continental style, although this is largely a matter of degree).

[101]It is indeed mainly the square ♮ that receives this treatment. Another manuscript displaying this scribal approach with consistency is the Eton Choirbook (**GB**-WRec 178).

Example 2: Parallel transcriptions of Dygon and Gaffurius proportion examples

a. *Supertripartiens septimas*

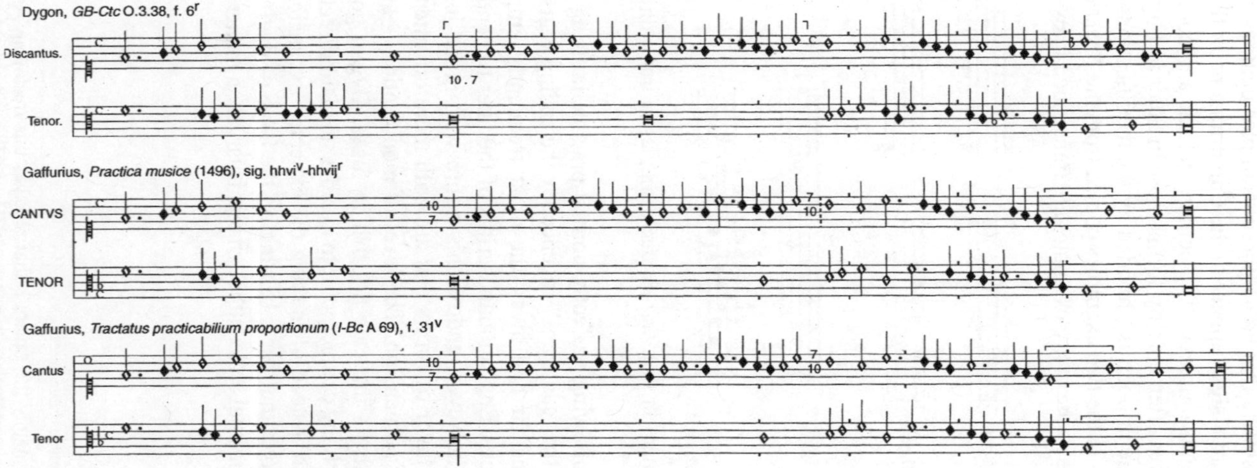

Example 2 (cont'd): Parallel transcriptions of Dygon and Gaffurius proportion examples

b. *Superquatripartiens quintas*

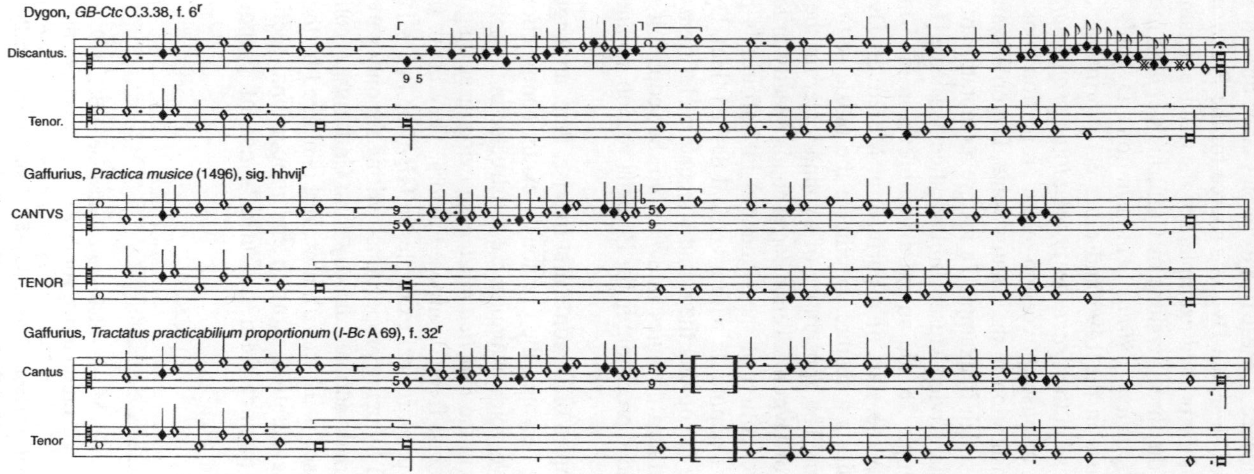

With the evidence of these two examples taken directly from Gaffurius's book, it becomes clear that Dygon's source for the *Practica music*e was, as expected, one of the printed exemplars of the treatise. Example 2 provides a comparison of the three versions of Gaffurius's *supertripartiens septimas* and *superquatripartiens quintas* demonstrations: Dygon's versions in **GB**-Ctc O.3.38; those in the 1496 and other early printings of the *Practica musice*; and those in the *Tractatus practabilium proportionum*, Gaffurius's pre-publication manuscript version of the proportion book.[102] In the major features of mensuration in the Cantus voice, Dygon's examples follow the printed pieces, which in example 2a feature a renotation of the Cantus in C time (in Bologna, Civico Museo Bibliografico Musicale [**I**-Bc], A69 it is in O) and in example 2b add an extra semibrevis in m. 5 to place the final cadence note at the start of a perfection. Moreover, Dygon's Tenor in example 2a reflects a feature specific to the music setting in the printed woodcut version. The appearance of a round ♭ clef for the first time in the ninth measure of Dygon's Tenor corresponds exactly in location to a line change (with repetition of the signature) in Gaffurius's printed example (represented in example 2a with a vertical dashed line). Dygon apparently saw no purpose in copying the round ♭ signature clef from Gaffurius's first line, which includes no notes in ♭-*fa*-♮-*mi*, but copied it when necessary with literal-minded precision; in the Bologna version, no line break occurs in the Tenor.

In the examples of Dygon's first treatise, then, an Anglicized approach marks both the new and the previously extant compositions. In the main, however, the two-voice examples are constructed in the spirit of Gaffurius's demonstrations in the *Practica musice*, showing discanting top voices using proportions against freely composed tenors. They break from the style of earlier English proportional examples in **GB**-Cmc Pepys 1236 and **GB**-Lbl Lansdowne 763 by using proportional writing for only part of each Discant line, a characteristic adopted directly from Gaffurius. A concrete distinction in conception (see p. 32 *supra*), however, is marked by the employment of the original mensuration signs to end proportional sections in Dygon's examples, as distinct from Gaffurius's use of proportions of lesser inequality.

[102]Bologna, Civico Museo Bibliografico Musicale (**I**-Bc), A69; see Christian Meyer, Giuliano Di Bacco, Pia Ernstbrunner, Alexander Rauch, and Cesarino Ruini, *The Theory of Music: Manuscripts from the Carolingian Era up to c.1500: Addenda, Corrigenda*, RISM BIII/6 (Munich: Henle, 2003), 453–55. I am indebted to Bonnie Blackburn for providing me with a reproduction of this manuscript.

There exists, moreover, in the first Cambridge treatise a type of example that is not to be found in Gaffurius's book and appears to have been of Dygon's own invention. Of the fifty-nine compositions in Dygon's first treatise, seven are three-voice works featuring two Discantus parts and one Tenor (see table 4 *infra*). The idea in these examples is to use the *genus multiplex* to create the more complex proportions of other *genera*, through the simultaneous use of two proportions. In the first such case, for example (f. 3^{r}, pp. 84–85 *infra*), the first Discantus goes into *quintupla* at the same time as the second Discantus uses *quadrupla*. The result is the execution of *sesquiquarta* (5:4) as the relation between the Discantus voices, while the only proportions performed by individual voices are of the *genus multiplex*. As with the examples of *inductiones*, Dygon is providing a simpler route to the performance of more difficult aspects of the theory. The fact that these compositions are for three voices, furthermore, confirms Dygon's basic idea of relating proportions to the music of the Tenor; otherwise, only two voices would be required, one for each simple proportion. A final noteworthy point in connection with these examples (see p. 23 *supra*) is the appearance of this type of writing in one of Dygon's works preserved outside **GB**-Ctc O.3.38. The three-voice *Rex benedicte*, transcribed in full in the Appendix, includes the following demonstration of *sesquitertia* (4:3) through the combination of *tripla* and *quadrupla* in m. 82, the only instance of proportional usage in Dygon's music surviving outside the treatises:

Example 3: Dygon, *Rex benedicte*, mm. 80–85 (**GB**-Lbl R.M. 24.d.2, ff. 165^{v}–166^{r})

Given that the segment of *quadrupla* could have been notated more easily as a simple run of semiminimae, the composer seems to have intended to highlight the superparticular relation between the voices at this point. Even in proportionally complex works (of which *Rex benedicte* is certainly not an example), the simultaneous employment of multiple proportions is exceptional; if the demonstration of such a usage in Dygon's treatise was intended to influence practical composition, it appears not to have had great effect.

As an aid to determining the general characteristics and development of the musical examples over the course of the treatises, table 4 lists all of the compositions in the manuscript with data on their basic features.

Table 4: Examples in **GB**-Ctc O.3.38

F.	# of voices	Proportions	Mensuration	Final[a]	Length[b] Breves	Semibreves	Proportion color
1^{r}	2	2:1 / 4:2	C	G	8	16	Red void
	2	2:1 / 4:2	O	G	8	24	Red full
1^{v}	2	3:1 / 9:3 / 6:2	O	G	6	18	Black void
	2	3:1 / 6:2 / 9:3	C	C	15.5	31	Red full
	2	4:1 / 8:2 / 12:3	O	G♭	8	24	Red full
2^{r}	2	5:1	C	C	6	12	Red full
	2	3:2 / 6:1 / 3:1 / 12:2	O	C	8	24	Red full
	2	7:1 / 14:2	C	D	8	16	Red full
2^{v}	2	8:1 / 16:2	C	D	8	16	Red full
	2	3:2 / 6:4 / 9:6	C	D♭	14	28	Red full
3^{r}	2	4:3 / 8:6	O	G♭/ D♭	4+4	12+12	Black full
	2	5:4 / 10:8	C	G	12	24	Red full
	3	5:1 / 4:1	C	C	6	12	Red full
3^{v}	2	6:5 / 12:10	C	G	10	20	Red full
	3	6:1 / 5:1	O	G(♭)	6	18	Red full
	2	7:6 / 14:12	C	G	10	20	Black void
4^{r}	3	7:1 / 3:2 / 6:1	C	C♭	6	12	Red full
	2	8:7	C	C	12	24	Red full
	3	8:1 / 7:1	C	F♭	8	16	Red full
4^{v}	2	9:8	C	C	16	32	Red void/ Red full
	3	3:2 / 9:2 / 4:1	C	F♭	8	16	Red full
5^{r}	2	5:3 / 10:6	O	C♭	8	24	Black void
	3	3:1 / 5:1	O	G♭	4	12	Red full
5^{v}	2	7:5	C	D♭	8	16	Red full
	2	9:7 / 4:1	C	G♭	12	24	Red full/ Red void
	2	7:4	C	D	8	16	Red full
	2	8:5	C	D	8	16	Red full
6^{r}	2	10:7	C	G	10	20	Red void
	2	9:5	O	D	7/7.33	21/22	Red full
	3	3:2 / 9:2 / 5:2	O	G	6	18	Red full

F.	# of voices	Proportions	Mensuration	Final[a]	Length[b] Breves	Semibreves	Proportion color
6^{v}	2	11:7	C	F♭	12	24	Black void
	2	13:9	O	G	6	18	Red full
	2	11:6	O	G	4	12	Red void
	2	12:7	C	D	8	16	Red full
7^{r}	2	13:7	C	D	8	16	Red full
	2	5:2	C	D	10	20	Red full
7^{v}	2	7:3	C	D	4	8	Red full
	2	9:4	C	D	12	24	Red full
	2	11:5	C	D	12	24	Red full
8^{r}	2	7:2	C	G	8	16	Red full
	2	10:3	C	D	8	16	Red full
	2	13:4	C	G	12	24	Red full
8^{v}	2	3:1 / 3:2 / 9:2	C	F♭	8	16	Red void/ Red full
	2	13:3	O	F♭	8	24	Red full
	2	17:4	C	C	8	16	Red full
9^{r}	2	11:2	C	D	8	16	Red full
	2	16:3	O	D	4	12	Red full
	2	21:4	C	G	8	16	Red full
9^{v}	2	8:3 / 16:6	C	C	12	24	Red full
10^{r}	2	12:5	O	D♭	6	18	Red full
	2	11:4	C	G	10	20	Red full
	2	13:5	O	C	6	18	Red full
10^{v}	2	11:3	C	D	10	20	Red full
	2	17:5	O	G	8	24	Red full
11^{r}	2	15:4	C	G♭	12	24	Red full
	2	18:5	O	G(♭)	6	18	Red full
11^{v}	2	14:3	C	C	8	16	Red full
	2	22:5	O	A(♭)	8	24	Red full
12^{r}	2	19:4	C	C	16	32	Red full
13^{r}	2	2:1 / 4:2	C	D♭	12	24	Red void
13^{v}	2	3:1	C	D♭	10	20	Red full
	2	9:3 / 3:1	C	D	10	20	Red full
14^{r}	2	4:1 / 8:2	C	G	10	20	Red void
	2	5:1	C	E	8	16	Red void
	2	6:1	C	F♭	8	16	Red full
14^{v}	2	8:1	O	F♭	6	18	Red full
	2	3:2 / 9:6	O	G(♭)	8	24	Red full
15^{r}	2	4:3	C	G	8	16	Black full
	2	5:4	C	C	16	32	Red full
15^{v}	2	6:5	O	D♭	8	24	Red full
	2	7:6	C	F♭	12	24	Red full
	2	8:7	C	G	16	32	Red full
16^{r}	2	9:8	O	D	8	24	Red full
	2	5:3	O	D♭	8	24	Red full

F.	# of voices	Proportions	Mensuration	Final[a]	Length[b] Breves	Semibreves	Proportion color
16^{v}	2	7:5	C	F♭	16	32	Red full
	2	5:2	C	F♭	16	32	Red full
17^{r}	2	7:3	O	F♭	12	36	Red full
	2	9:4	O	G	9.33	28	Red void
17^{v}	2	7:2	C	D(♭)	16	32	Red full
	2	3:2 / 9:2 / 3:1	O	D♭	12	36	Red full
18^{r}	2	8:3	O	F♭	12	36	Red full

[a]The ♭ following the letter of the final indicates the presence of a ♭ signature clef; signature in one voice or one section of the composition only is indicated with parentheses.

[b]Lengths do not include final notes.

The tabulated data invite several observations concerning distinctive characteristics of the compositions. In the first instance, it is immediately apparent that Dygon's examples are almost without exception organized into an even number of breves; it would appear that Dygon kept track of rhythmic organization at the *modus* level, a structure not present in Gaffurius's examples. The three exceptions (on ff. 1^{v}, 6^{r} and 17^{r}) each conclude in mid-brevis (in at least one voice) but are otherwise stylistically similar to the rest. The case on f. 6^{r} can be explained through the fact that it is one of the examples adapted from Gaffurius (although the extension into a mid-brevis ending is Dygon's work). The other two instances are more difficult to understand; if they do not represent mere oversights on the composer's part, perhaps their symmetrical positioning points to an enigmatic organizational principle for the entire set of examples.[103]

In terms of tonal characteristics, we find an equal number of examples with finals on D and G, by far the best represented finals with twenty-seven examples each—nearly a third each of the eighty-two total. If the examples on G with a round ♭ signature clef are grouped together with the D examples, this *protus* tonality comes out most frequently. F and C are used twelve and fourteen times respectively; with the round ♭ clef excluding two of the examples on C from a *tritus* group, we again find a balance, of twelve and twelve. E is used only once as a final—is it there for the sake of completeness?—but the single example on A accompanies it in a *deuterus* grouping through the use of the round ♭. The frequent appearance of con-

[103]The examples are the fourth from the beginning and the end of the book. It may be notable in this respect as well that the exceptional second example on f. 6^{r} stands at the midpoint of Treatise 1, being the thirtieth of sixty examples (treating the *sesquitertia* demonstrations on f. 3^{r} as two examples).

secutive pairs or larger groups of examples with the same final reinforces an impression of sequential design, if only at a local level.

Similar pairings of examples present themselves through very obvious but limited motivic relations: for instance, the Tenors of the first and second examples open with the same pitch material, while the second and third examples are linked through the opening of the Discantus voice. Such reuse of opening motives occurs frequently and not only in consecutive groups (compare, for example, the Tenors of f. 1^{v}, first example, and f. 4^{r}, first example; or both voices in f. 8^{v}, first example, and f. 10^{r}, third example). A single example of complete reuse of a voice part occurs in the Tenor of the two examples on f. 13^{v} (which was clearly composed originally to accompany the simple monorhythmic scale in the Discantus of the first of these examples).

Imitation is in general rare and usually carried out in only the briefest of motives—often little more than a characteristic interval, only recognizable as a vague type of imitation because of placement at the opening of a composition or after a rest in each voice. This approach to imitative writing is, of course, wholly in line with the large-scale English "festal" style of the early sixteenth century, which did not yet show as much influence from continental structural imitation as did certain types of less ostentatious sacred and secular polyphony. While bearing this assessment in mind, however, it is nevertheless possible to detect an increase in cases of imitation toward the end of the book, with a more assured handling: witness the transparent passages of imitation at the 5th in the first examples of ff. 15^{v} and 17^{v}. If the late appearance of such writing in **GB**-Ctc O.3.38 says nothing about broad chronology—such pseudo-canonic imitation appears frequently in later fifteenth-century polyphony, particularly for two or three voices—, it offers support for the idea that the composer worked sequentially through material as it stands today. Against the festal compositional style of ca. 1500, as well, one may judge the treatment of dissonance in Dygon's counterpoint: uncomfortably free by the standards of a Tinctoris or Gaffurius, with its occasional "appoggiatura"-style dissonances and dissonant leaps, the writing in the examples is more acceptable by late fifteenth-century English standards. Contrapuntal crudities that are undeniably present, both in the theoretical examples and in Dygon's other compositions, hint at some inexperience as a composer, but by no means the type of incompetence encountered in certain earlier English proportion examples.[104]

---

[104]See p. 5 *supra*. For several representative examples of compositional blemishes in Dygon's works, see: f. 1^{v}, first example, m. 2 (p. 73 *infra*); f. 10^{r}, second example, mm. 1–2 (p. 125 *infra*); and *Rex benedicte*, m. 39 (see Appendix).

Considered together, the examples of the book attest to a unified compositional approach. The lack of any distinction between the type of writing encountered in the first and second treatises strongly suggests the hand of a single theorist and composer throughout the whole manuscript, an impression that will be reinforced by the investigation of the second treatise. Vague hints at a numerological organization, including a careful balance of tonalities employed in different pieces, may reveal a concern for deliberate design spanning both treatises as one whole; but it is difficult to adhere to any strict numerical interpretation, and a general desire to employ simple ratios on a large scale need not produce a specific mathematical scheme.

Treatise 2: An Alternative System for Notating Proportions

There can be little doubt that the second treatise of the Cambridge manuscript, ff. 13^r–18^r (pp. 136–59 *infra*), was intended as a companion to the first. With the basics of proportional usage in mensural notation laid out in the first treatise, the shorter second section of the book repeats the traversal of the proportional *genera* in order but can afford to leave out all definitions and introductory material.[105] Excepting several groups of proportions left out of the second treatise (*superbipartiens septimas* through *supersexcupartiens septimas*, *dupla sesquiquinta*, *tripla sesquitertia*, *tripla sesquiquarta*, *quadrupla sesquitertia* through *quintupla sesquiquarta*, and *dupla superbipartiens quintas* through *quadrupla supertripartiens quartas*), the text follows the same format in exactly the same style as the first treatise. The musical examples (all for two voices) likewise display no stylistic compositional features distinguishing them from those in the first section. In essence, the treatise offers an abbreviated reference list—with musical examples—of proportions notated with a new and unusual system.

The central idea of the proportional notation system expounded in the treatise is the translation of mensuration signs (C, O, ☉̶, ⊙, Ɔ)[106] into numerical values that can be treated arithmetically and compared. No explanation of the system's principles is provided in the manuscript; each proportion is merely demonstrated with one or more combinations of mensuration signs. Nevertheless, the simple derivation of the combinations of signs from the proportions is easily enough observed without a separate exposi-

[105] A single exception is the treatment of the first proportion, *dupla*, which includes a partial and nearly meaningless excerpt from the definition in the first treatise ("in qua [*sc.* proportione dupla] maior notularum numerus aequiualet minori"); see pp. 136–37 *infra*.

[106] The use of the signs ⦶ and Ↄ̇ in the treatise is a special case that falls outside the main system; see pp. 51–52 *infra*.

tion; a listing of all the groupings used to show proportions in the second treatise can be found in table 5.

Table 5: Structure of second treatise

Proportion	Shown with:	Notes
Dupla	C Ɔ 4 C C C C	Incomplete definition given (partial re-copying of the definition from first treatise)
Tripla	Φ Ͽ ⊙ Ͼ	Two examples
Quadrupla	C Ɔ C 8 C	
Quintupla	O Ɔ C	Always *per semibrevem*
Sextupla	CC Ɔ C	Always *per semibrevem*
Septupla	CO Ɔ C	No example given ("Septupla raro aut nunquam in usu est"); always *per semibrevem*
Octupla	CC Ɔ CC	[Always] *per semibrevem*
Sesquialtera	O C ⊙ O Ͼ C	
Sesquitertia	Ɔ C Ͼ C	Example only uses Ɔ; second method mentioned after example only for completeness
Sesquiquarta	OC CC Ͼ C C C	Statement that *sesquiquarta* and all following superparticular proportions are not in use
Sesquiquinta	O O O C Ͼ ϾC Ͼ	
Sesquisexta	CϾ CC C C	
Sesquiseptima	CC CϾ CC C	
Sesquioctaua	⊙ CC CC	

Superbipartiens tertias	OC O	
	ϾC Ͼ	
Superbipartiens quintas	CO C OC	
	CϾ C ϾC	
Dupla sesquialtera	OC C	
	ϾC C	
Dupla sesquitertia	CϾ C Ͼ	
	CO C O	
Dupla sesquiquarta	⊙ C C	
Tripla sesquialtera	CO C C	
	CϾ C C	
Quadrupla sesquialtera	O C	
	⊙ C	
Dupla superbipartiens tertias	CC CC O	
	CC CC Ͼ	
	8 O	
	8 Ͼ	

The arithmetic system in operation here is in most instances perfectly straightforward. Each mensuration sign receives a value, dependent upon whether it represents a perfect or imperfect mensuration (considering only the semibrevis-brevis and minima-semibrevis relationships); an imperfect sign is worth two minimae or semibreves and a perfect sign three. The sign Ɔ represents the one semibrevis; ⊙, which is perfect on both levels, translates to nine minimae (the number of minimae in a brevis under that mensuration). The values of signs grouped together are added together to yield a final value for a group.

As an example, consider the two ways of notating *dupla sesquialtera* (5:2) presented in the treatise (f. 16v; p. 152 *infra*). To notate the proportion at the level of the semibrevis, the group OC is compared to a single C. There are three semibreves to the brevis under the mensuration O and two under the mensuration C. Converting the groups to their arithmetic values, then, we have: (O + C : C) = (3 + 2 : 2) = (5 : 2). At the level of the minima, on the other hand, the grouping is ϾC : C. Under Ͼ, there are three minimae to the semibrevis; under C, there are two minimae to the semibrevis. Therefore, the resulting conversion is: (Ͼ + C : C) = (3 + 2 : 2) = (5 : 2).

The availability of different groups of signs to represent the same proportion, thus, has the advantage of allowing the notator to encode more information than is possible with the standard Hindu-Arabic numeral system: each ratio is signaled as applying at the level of either the semibrevis or the minima. Instead of merely 5:2, we have 5 semibreves : 2 semibreves or 5 minimae : 2 minimae. Dygon had already displayed a concern for this distinction on the opening pages of the first treatise, where three of the first four examples have "per minimam" or "per semibrevem" written on or near the staves (f. 1^{r-v}, pp. 70–73 *infra*). In the second treatise, the extremely economical text makes frequent mention of which rhythmic levels are demonstrated and acceptable, as for example in the warning "Quintupla semper per semibrevem" (which also applies to *sextupla*, *septupla*, and *octupla*). Of course, the fact that the signs of minor prolation (O and C) are used for proportions at the level of both the semibrevis and the minima leads to cases of ambiguity, where context must aid in determining values. For example, in the one instance where O is used in a proportion at the level of the minima, it is worth six minimae (*sesquialtera*, ⊙ : O = 9 : 6; f. 14^{v}, pp. 144–45 *infra*);[107] in nearly all other cases, at the level of the semibrevis, O is worth three semibreves. The other exception arises problematically in the notation of *quadrupla sesquialtera* (9:2) in semibreves, since the single sign O is used to represent the value of nine semibreves: the text explains that this is because the sign is meant to imply perfect (minor) *modus* as well as *tempus*.[108] Unfortunately, the resulting set of signs, O : C, has already been used to represent *sesquialtera* (3:2),[109] since O at the level of the semibrevis is given the value of three semibreves everywhere else in the treatise.

Several other cases that stand outside the regular system presented in the treatise offer less difficulty, as they are obvious exceptions. The four instances of mensuration signs being compared to Hindu-Arabic numerals (4:C, 8:C, 8:O, 8:Ͼ) are straightforward and confirm the numerical interpretation of mensuration signs explained above.[110] The proportion *sesquitertia* (4:3) is demonstrated with the symbol Ↄ alone, a usage that was standard both in English and continental theory and practice (even if it was criticized

---

[107]It would appear that for this particular representation of *sesquialtera*, the value was determined by the number of minimae in a brevis as opposed to the number of minimae in a semibrevis.

[108]F. 17^{v}, pp. 156–57 *infra*.

[109]F. 14^{v}, pp. 144–45 *infra*.

[110]Ff. 13^{r}, 14^{r}, 18^{r}; pp. 136–37, 140–41, 158–59, and 172 (plate 2) *infra*.

by some).[111] The Cambridge treatise points out with regard to this example—probably with prescriptive intent, to judge by the similar treatment of the *sesquitertia* example in the first treatise—that the notes of the *sesquitertia* section are in the coloration black full, a concern that is not otherwise addressed in the manuscript. The only other exceptions are the symbols Φ and Ɔ, used individually to indicate *tripla* at the level of the semibrevis and minima, respectively.[112] With regard to the sign Φ in general use, there is considerable ambiguity (and no current scholarly consensus) surrounding its exact effect in fifteenth- and early sixteenth-century practice; certainly a simple indication of *tripla* is not among the standard interpretations of the sign.[113] The example in the Cambridge manuscript, however, does happen to correspond to one of the secure uses of Φ: when used *simultaneously* with voices in other mensurations, the sign indicates diminution by half (and *tempus perfectum*).[114] Since the example in **GB**-Ctc O.3.38 is in C, the appearance of Φ with this meaning, assuming equality of the brevis, would cause two breves in *tempus perfectum* (in the affected voice) to equal one brevis of *tempus imperfectum* (in the other voice)—in other words, six semibreves under Φ are equal to two under C, which is in fact *tripla*. The other sign for *tripla*, Ɔ, is not unknown in English compositions of the period: examples include the first Gloria-Credo pair of the "York Masses" and the *Missa Ave maria* of Thomas Ashwell.[115]

---

[111]F. 15^{r}, pp. 144–45 *infra*; Gaffurius, *Practica musice*, sig. $ggvi^{v}$. For an English theoretical demonstration of Ɔ as *sesquitertia*, see the treatise *Proporcio est 2orum numerorum* in **GB**-Lbl Lansdowne 763, ff. 123^{v}–124^{r}.

[112]F. 13^{v}, pp. 138–39 *infra*.

[113]For examples of the discussion surrounding the meanings and effects of Φ, see Rob C. Wegman, "What Is 'acceleratio mensurae'?" *Music and Letters* 73 (1992): 515–24; Berger, *Mensuration and Proportion Signs*, 125–39; Margaret Bent, "The Early Use of the Sign Φ," *Early Music* 24 (1996): 199–225; Rob C. Wegman, "Different Strokes for Different Folks? On Tempo and Diminution in Fifteenth-Century Music," *Journal of the American Musicological Society* 53 (2000): 461–505; and responding in the same issue, Margaret Bent, "On the Interpretation of Φ in the Fifteenth Century," *Journal of the American Musicological Society* 53 (2000): 597–612.

[114]Bent, "The Early Use," 219.

[115]**GB**-Ybi Mus. 1, ff. 5^{v}–6^{r} (no published edition); and **GB**-Ob Mus. Sch. e.376–81, no. 13. On the use of proportions in the latter, see Woodley, *John Tucke*, 112–21. A later didactic example from Morley's *Plaine and easie introduction*, a lengthy proportional composition entitled *Christes crosse*, uses *tripla* under Ɔ (with and without the numerals 3 1). Morley's discussion brings up the confusion of *sextupla* and *tripla* mentioned in Dygon's treatise (see p. 36 *supra*): "The first change which cometh after the Proportion of equality is commonly called Sextupla, or six to one, signified by the More Prolation retorted thus …. But if we consider rightly, that which we call Sextupla is but true Tripla

The system expounded in the second Cambridge treatise, thus, follows a regular and discernible order, with certain exceptions granted as concessions to known usages. Did the idea of this process of arithmetic translation, however, arise out of the blue? Was it Dygon's invention, intended as a personal contribution to complement the Gaffurian theory of the first treatise? The surviving musical sources offer no indication that the system ever found real practical use. Only a single set of compositions in Baldwin's Commonplace Book displays anything approaching the combinations of mensuration signs in **GB**-Ctc O.3.38.[116] These are works that were clearly included and grouped together as examples of unusual and extreme proportional writing, perhaps with some didactic intent; as far as the details of usage are concerned, however, no clear system like that of the Cambridge treatise is discernible (figure 2).

Figure 2: **GB**-Lbl R.M. 24.d.2, f. 103^{r} (detail)[117]

There is, however, one theoretical manuscript that offers some measure of corroboration for the system in Treatise 2 and possibly a source for the idea. Among the miscellaneous items brought together in the notebook assembled by John Tucke (**GB**-Lbl Add. 10336) are various texts dealing with proportions in music. Apart from the treatise by John Hothby

---

pricked in black notes; but because I made it to express Sextupla I have set it down in semibreves, allowing six for a stroke and taking away the retorted Mood" (Morley, *A Plaine and Easy Introduction* [ed. Harman], 85). The section Morley describes equates six black minimae with two preceding white minimae (or three black semibreves with one preceding white semibrevis) and so can only be described as *sextupla* through the comparison of six minimae to one semibrevis criticized by Dygon.

[116] **GB**-Lbl R.M. 24.d.2, ff. 100^{v}–115^{r}.

[117] Nathaniel Giles, *Miserere* ("a lesson of descant of thirtie eighte propocions: [*sic*] of sundrie kindes: made by m^{r} giles m^{r} of the children of windsor then: & now m^{r} of þ^{e} children of þ^{e} chappell also:"). The groupings demonstrated here are: Ↄ⃒ = 2:5; ↃↃ = 4:5; Ↄ⃒ = 8:1; ⊙ = 2:7; ⊙Ↄ = 4:7; ⊙ↃↃ = 8:7.

(*Proportiones secundum ioannem otteby*) and other purely arithmetical discussions of proportion, notes on the proportions represented by unusual notational colors, and various other such texts,[118] we find on f. 100r–v a particularly relevant discussion.[119] After a section on the proportions caused by various combinations of mensurations and colors (black, red, and blue only) appears a paragraph beginning "Item ad cognoscendum proportiones per figuras que uocantur circuli." This section, already connected terminologically to the second Cambridge treatise by associating proportions with "circuli," lists a number of proportional relations between mensuration signs with a level of correspondence too high to be coincidental. In table 6, the proportional relations explained in this section of Tucke's notebook are listed.

Table 6: Means of indicating proportions through mensuration signs, **GB**-Lbl Add. 10336, f. 100v

Proportion	**Shown with**[a]
Sesquialtera (3:2)	⊙ ○
	Ċ C
	Ↄ̇ Ċ
	○ ⌽
	Ↄ̸̇ C
Dupla (2:1)	C Ↄ
Subsesquialtera (2:3)	C ○
Sesquitertia (4:3)	Ↄ Ↄ ○
Tripla (3:1)	Ↄ̇ 3 C
Superbipartiens tertias (5:3)	○ C ○
Quadrupla (4:1)	Ↄ Ↄ C

[a]Sign groups that match the corresponding examples in **GB**-Ctc O.3.38 exactly are indicated with dark shading; inexact matches with a clear relation to the system in **GB**-Ctc O.3.38 (see below) receive light shading.

In the signs of *sesquialtera, dupla*, and *superbipartiens tertias*, Tucke's text includes combinations that are encountered exactly in the Cambridge text. The grouping for *subsesquialtera*, moreover, fits unproblematically into

[118]Woodley, *John Tucke*, 50–53 and 57.

[119]Edited and translated ibid., 68–71, with a discussion at 121–22.

Dygon's additive system of translation, with C : O translating to 2 semibreves : 3 semibreves (recall that the Cambridge manuscript includes no examples or discussion of any such proportions of lesser inequality). For the indications of *sesquitertia* and *quadrupla*, the text in **GB**-Lbl Add. 10336 seems to employ a system that reverses the roles of C and Ɔ encountered in **GB**-Ctc O.3.38: instead of CC : O, we have ƆƆ : O (*sesquitertia*); and in place of CC : Ɔ, there is ƆƆ : C (*quadrupla*). Given that the treatment of these two signs in **GB**-Lbl Add. 10336 for *dupla*, *subsesquialtera*, and *superbipartiens tertias* matches the usage in **GB**-Ctc O.3.38, there is an inconsistency of approach here that is not altogether uncharacteristic of Tucke's notebook. Moreover, there are several groupings in *sesquialtera* and *tripla* that bear no readily discernible relation to a main system—just as the Cambridge manuscript includes a number of exceptional cases seemingly based on traditional practice. If the number of conflicting details in the theoretical discussions in Tucke's manuscript can be attributed to a process of gradual compilation out of numerous sources and university lectures, we can perhaps posit the existence of various earlier states of the proportional theory under discussion. In the basic concept of performing arithmetic operations on mensuration signs ("circles"), at least, the texts of Dygon and Tucke are in agreement. Without Dygon's version, however, it would be difficult to make sense of the cases mentioned in Tucke's manuscript, and Ronald Woodley's discussion of the latter interprets the proportional relationships as occurring between durations of notes under the different mensuration signs ("C : O = 2 : 3 implies breve equivalence," etc.).[120] This reading passes over in silence the groupings that correspond to no known mensural usage, i.e., OC and ƆƆ. The musical examples in **GB**-Ctc O.3.38 demonstrate that the situation may not be quite so sophisticated: rather than explaining proportional relationships that occur through the simultaneous or successive application of different mensurations, we are perhaps dealing with a simple notational alternative to the Hindu-Arabic numeral system of proportions, the additive system elaborated fully in Dygon's treatise. The meanings of these individual signs in mensural usage provide the explanation for their values in this system of proportional notation, but as indicators of proportions they cannot function here as mensuration signs. Indeed, Tucke's text makes no mention of mensuration in this passage: the incipit could be paraphrased as "Likewise, in order to recognize/identify propor-

[120]Ibid., 122.

tions through the signs that are called circles ....”[121] Such an interpretation removes much of the difficulty in Tucke’s statements, even if certain combinations of signs remain mysterious (and decidedly absent from practical sources).

It hardly needs emphasizing that the proportional system encountered in the second Dygon treatise, and in a more fragmented state in **GB**-Lbl Add. 10336, by no means conforms to orthodox notational practice. Such an employment of mensuration signs, in combinations of up to seven symbols, divorced from any effect on relative rhythmic divisions, is unknown in continental theory. It must be noted, furthermore, that the idea is not encountered elsewhere in the English theoretical tradition, which in its treatment of proportions was generally in line with international practice.[122] The limitation of this peculiar system to **GB**-Ctc O.3.38 and **GB**-Lbl Add. 10336 may, in fact, suggest a set of close chronological and institutional boundaries. As the only surviving English theory manuscripts definitely datable to the early Tudor period, these two books represent a stage in the development of English musical thought that is otherwise traceable mainly through the comparison of earlier and later writings.[123] For the set of notes on f. 100 of Tucke’s book, we can arrive at a specific copying period of 1504–1507, which corresponds to the time when Tucke was studying for the degree of M.A. at New College, Oxford.[124] While the surviving manuscript of Dygon’s treatises can be dated to a later period, the book offers no explicit clues to the date when the treatises might have originally been written; the *terminus post quem* of 1496 (the printing of the *Practica music*e) is followed by several decades that could have seen the compilation of Dygon’s texts. It may be of no little significance, however, that Dygon studied at Oxford in the period shortly after Tucke’s departure, supplicating for the B.Mus. in 1512.[125] In the two surviving English sources of proportional music theory from the early sixteenth century, we may well have examples of musical teaching deriving directly from an Oxonian milieu.

---

[121]Woodley’s translation reads “Likewise, in order to discover the meanings of proportions through the signs which are called circles” (ibid., 71).

[122]With certain other exceptions; see pp. 4–7 *supra*.

[123]For a more detailed discussion, see Dumitrescu, “Early Tudor Music Theory and the International Traditions,” chapter 4 in “Anglo-Continental Musical Relations.”

[124]See the explicits on ff. 73^{v} and 104^{v}, with Woodley’s explanations: *John Tucke*, 50–52 and 57.

[125]See p. 15 *supra*.

The idea that the theory of Dygon's second treatise is connected to a particular university tradition is attractive but purely speculative. The little we can guess about the role of *musica practica* in a course at Oxford during this period is mainly dependent upon the evidence of Tucke's notebook. The final requirements of the university for a music degree, as mentioned above, involved the setting of one or two large-scale compositions. We have no evidence that a theory manuscript such as **GB-**Ctc O.3.38 could act as a substitute for a composition exercise; moreover, the existence of the three-voice fragments in Baldwin's Commonplace Book indicates that substantial liturgical works by Dygon did once circulate. At best, we can posit that the theory of Dygon's second treatise draws upon material the monk could have encountered during his student days at Oxford, if it was not more widespread in English teaching at the time—something that can be neither confirmed nor denied, given the lack of sources.

It is clear, in any case, that the second Cambridge treatise was not assembled prior to the author's contact with the *Practica musice*. The use of Gaffurius's book as the structural basis for the first treatise, and as the inspiration for its style of examples, is repeated in the second treatise. It is perfectly plausible that the second treatise, in fact, draws directly on the first treatise rather than Gaffurius's text, in that it treats a subset of the cases from the first treatise, which in turn is a subset of the cases in the *Practica musice*. Whether directly or indirectly, however, the Italian work lies at the source of the each of the two English treatises. For determining the original milieu of Dygon's writing, this fact does little to reconcile the treatises with the musician's Oxonian years. His one documented journey to the Continent was his period of study, supposedly at Paris and Leuven, around a decade following the supplication at Oxford; and there is, apart from Dygon's own work, no indication that Gaffurius's work was known at an English university at this time. Nevertheless, we should not underestimate the capability of theory prints to travel widely to university towns, as demonstrated in the quick appearance in Oxford of books by Ornithoparcus and Wollick.[126] If we do not have to rely on Dygon's continental sojourn as the source of his encounter with the *Practica musice*, then the evidence for the treatises' origins remains inconclusive.

Our investigation of the treatises and Dygon's biography can lead to numerous conclusions; a distinction must be observed, however, between the dating of the treatises and the dating of the Cambridge manuscript, which may well represent a late copy of the material. It is clear in the first place

---

[126]See pp. 11–12 *supra.*

that the current form of the treatises, as the only material contained in **GB**-Ctc O.3.38, is to some extent a formal state of presentation by comparison with the miscellaneous "notebook" approach encountered in Tucke's manuscript. A number of impressions derived from the investigation of the texts are reinforced by the physical characteristics of the manuscript described in the following section:

- The Cambridge book represents a fair copy of the treatises
- The book was assembled specifically for these two works alone
- A single scribe (not a professional) copied the entire book, probably over a short period of time
- The manuscript stayed in Canterbury in the sixteenth century but did not form part of the library at St. Augustine's

The idea that the two treatises, with their closely related texts and musical style, were designed to be used together suggests that if Dygon was not the author-editor of the second treatise, it was the work of someone consciously emulating the first text. As an example of a unified work of some brevity, even with both treatises combined, the material in **GB**-Ctc O.3.38 can, however, be ascribed more comfortably to a single musician. The major contribution of Dygon in the first treatise is the set of musical examples interspersed throughout the text; the format of the teaching and examples belongs to Gaffurius. It may be the case, therefore, that the first text was intended mainly as an introductory exposition, positioned to prepare the reader for the particularities of the second treatise. It is certain that the second treatise expects of the reader an understanding of the material explicated in the first treatise: the amount of explanatory text regarding proportions is kept to an absolute minimum. The notational system demonstrated in this second text was particularly English, perhaps even peculiar to the teaching encountered at Oxford University. Dygon's exposition of the system, however, extends it well beyond the realm of practical use. Is the writer's admission of this fact an indication that the text was intended for the pseudo-speculative context of *musica practica* teaching at university, as known from the idiosyncratic theory of Tucke's manuscript? Once again we are back in Oxford: this hypothesis, which would place the creation of the treatises probably at some point in the early 1510s to coincide with Dygon's time at Oxford, has much to commend it in consideration of the stylistic aspects of the musical examples.[127] The latest surviving sources to combine red and black as their

[127]It was probably a similar speculation that led Frank Harrison to date the manuscript to ca. 1510 ("Music at Oxford," 358). Although the treatises themselves may date

basic notational colors are the most formal English choirbooks and songbooks of the first quarter of the sixteenth century or slightly earlier,[128] during which years simple black void notation was coming into greater use. **GB-**Ctc O.3.38 seems to stand in the middle, as a small and formal but non-professional source, employing black void as the basic notational color but with frequent use of red notation. In the abundant use of square ♮ and round ♭ signs in places where they are obviously superfluous, the Cambridge book agrees most closely with the Eton Choirbook; similar habits are encountered in other English books of these years but with a lesser frequency of usage. The general contrapuntal style of Dygon's examples, moreover, fits into the type of writing associated with the large-scale festal polyphony of the late fifteenth and early sixteenth century; the florid passage-work in semiminimae and fusae encountered in numerous examples recalls the Eton style rather than an advanced work of the late 1520s such as Taverner's *Mater cristi* or even the typical music of Fayrfax and his contemporaries.[129]

If the stylistic aspects of the music suggest Dygon's university years as the most likely time for the composition of the treatises, we must nevertheless avoid assuming that this speculation provides a context for the Cambridge manuscript as well. The paleographical evidence (see "The Manuscript" *infra*) points to Canterbury as the book's likely area of circulation in the sixteenth century. Furthermore, to the reservations expressed above regarding the association of the book with any specific university program can be added the observation that even the contents of Tucke's book—securely associated as they are with a university figure—were known outside that context. In addition to the copy of Tucke's book made by William Chelle at Hereford, the theory section of the earlier and probably monastic book **GB-**Cmc Pepys 1236 shares many of its unusual texts with the Tucke manuscript.[130] The prospect therefore that Dygon's treatises were intended for use in the learned setting of St. Augustine's need not be discarded, nor of course should university and monastic use of the treatises

---

from this period, a much later dating for the surviving book is proposed below ("The Manuscript").

[128]Well-known examples are **GB-**WRec 178; **GB-**Lbl 5465; Cambridge, University Library (**GB-**Cu), Nn. 6. 46; **GB-**Llp 1; and Cambridge, Gonville and Caius College (**GB-**Cgc), 667.

[129]See, for example, the compositions on f. 16^{r-v}, pp. 150–53 *infra*.

[130]Woodley, *John Tucke*, 66. On the origin and dating of **GB-**Cmc Pepys 1236, see Sydney R. Charles, "The Provenance and Dates of the Pepys Ms. 1236," *Musica disciplina* 16 (1962): 57–71; and Frank Ll. Harrison, "Music for the Sarum Rite: MS. 1236 in the Pepys Library, Magdalene College, Cambridge," *Annales musicologiques* 6 (1958–63): 99–144.

be considered mutually exclusive. An important reason for sending promising young monks to the centers of higher education was presumably the eventual intellectual benefit of the entire house.

With regard to the Cambridge book, it may be of only limited significance that the treatises themselves were most likely composed in the early years of the sixteenth century. Theoretical writings enjoyed a much greater longevity at this period than did polyphonic compositions in general, and a style that would seem hopelessly out of date in a practical source would not necessarily be viewed as such in a treatise. If the Cambridge manuscript, as seems likely, was copied as late as the 1540s (see below), when St. Augustine's was no more and Dygon had been pensioned off with the rest of the religious, the material would still be of relevance. The proportional compositions of Baldwin's book, many from the late sixteenth century, and the remarks in Morley's treatise indicate clearly that at least some practitioners retained a healthy interest in the subject to the end of the century and beyond. No other writer in Dygon's day achieved, however, such a remarkable synthesis of mainstream continental teaching with the idiosyncracies of English practice, at a period when the English were just developing their taste for "whatsoever cometh from beyond the seas (and specially from Italy)."[131]

The Manuscript

C

Cambridge, Trinity College, O.3.38

Parchment (some flyleaves paper); iv+i+18+ii+ii ff., 245×200 mm.
England; ca. 1540

1. John Dygon, ⟨Proportiones practicabiles secundum gaffurium⟩. *Inc.*: "De Genere multiplici et eius speciebus…" *Exp.*: "… ut hoc precipitur concentu. Quod Joannes Dygonus Modo Vuylborus." (ff. 1^{r}–12^{r}; f. 12^{v} blank)

2. [John Dygon], ⟨Tractatus secundus⟩. *Inc.*: "Proportio dupla est prima species multiplicis generis…" *Exp.*: "… Duplasuperbipartienstercias per semibreuem ut hic CCCC ad O aut hoc pacto per minimam ut hic CCCC ad ⋶ aut per figuram ut hic . 8 ad O . 8 ad ⋶ ." (ff. 13^{r}–18^{r}; 18^{v} blank)

131 Morley, *A Plain and Easy Introduction* (ed. Harman), 293.

This slim volume, composed of parchment sheets of irregular quality and thickness, is dedicated solely to the treatises edited here. The original corpus of the book is structured as two gatherings, as depicted in figure 3.

Figure 3: Gathering structure of **GB**-Ctc O.3.38

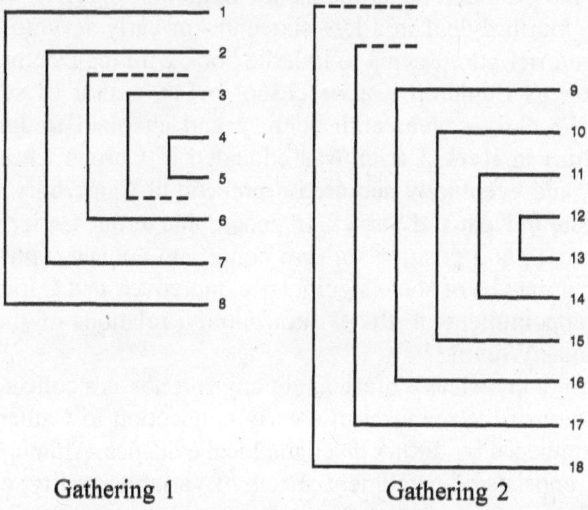

The manuscript's structure excludes any possibility that the two treatises were originally separate and merely bound together at a later date (since the first treatise continues into gathering 2). It may be the case, however, that the final two folios (17 and 18) were appended one at a time to the second gathering as the scribe filled his space but knew there was too little material to justify a third gathering. In any case, the book was almost certainly a complete self-contained unit from the start, made specifically for the Dygon treatises. There are no indications that the manuscript ever suffered any losses (apart from minor trimming at several margins) or underwent any significant structural changes when re-bound into its modern cardboard covers.

The fifth flyleaf contains various pressmarks: "N°: 98," "B.32.," "B.15.33," and "O.3.38." The last of these is the present pressmark; none matches the system used in the library of St. Augustine's.[132] The B shelfmarks have been struck through, but the "B.32." mark corresponds to the "N°: 98" mark in an ordering of books donated to Trinity College in 1738 by Robert Gale from the substantial library collected by his father Dr. Thomas Gale and himself; these marks are found in the volumes that now comprise

---

[132] See James, *The Ancient Libraries*.

most of the O collection at Trinity College.[133] The fact that **GB**-Ctc O.3.38 cannot be identified in the catalogue of the Gale collection printed in 1697 suggests that it was acquired by the family between that time and the donation four decades later.[134] Few further clues survive as to the book's early history, the most explicit being the name "Beniamin Charier" written on the front of the fourth flyleaf in a late sixteenth- or early seventeenth-century hand.[135] The inscription seems to link the book with the Doctor of Divinity known better as Benjamin Carier (1566–1614), author of several tracts printed in the early seventeenth century and chaplain to James I from 1603.[136] Born in Kent, Carier was educated at Corpus Christi College, Cambridge, and eventually acquired a prebend at Canterbury; his earliest benefices were in Kent and Sussex. In geographic terms, Carier's biography places him in a good position to have come into contact with the book at Canterbury; it may be of some significance, moreover, that Carier owed several of his appointments to the Wotton family, relations of John Dygon's friend Nicholas Wotton.[137]

Carier is not known as a musician of any sort nor as a collector of books. The conjecture of the manuscript's early connection to Canterbury, however, is strengthened by further paleographical evidence. Although the manuscript body consists of parchment sheets of variable quality, certain front and back flyleaves are paper; two of these sheets contain watermarks, reproduced in figure 4.

---

[133] James, *The Western Manuscripts*, 3:v–xiii.

[134] Edward Bernard, *Catalogi librorum manuscriptorum Anglie et Hibernie*, 2 vols. (Oxford: Theatrum Sheldonianum, 1697), 2/1:185–95.

[135] Not "Breuiarium Charier," as in James, *The Western Manuscripts*, 3:220.

[136] Michael Questier, "Crypto-Catholicism, Anti-Calvinism and Conversion at the Jacobean Court: The Enigma of Benjamin Carier," *Journal of Ecclesiastical History* 47 (1996): 45–64; *Dictionary of National Biography*, 3:989–90. The "Charier" form of the surname appears in his first print, from 1606, whereas the later books use "Carier": *A Short-Title Catalogue of Books Printed in England, Scotland, & Ireland and of English Books Printed Abroad. 1475–1640*, 3 vols., 2d ed. by W. A. Jackson, F. S. Ferguson, and Katherine F. Pantzer (London: The Bibliographical Society, 1976–91), 1:207, no. 4622.

[137] Questier, "Crypto-Catholicism," 49, n. 15. On Dygon's relation to Wotton, see pp. 21–22 *supra*.

Figure 4: Watermarks in flyleaves of **GB**-Ctc O.3.38

a. b.

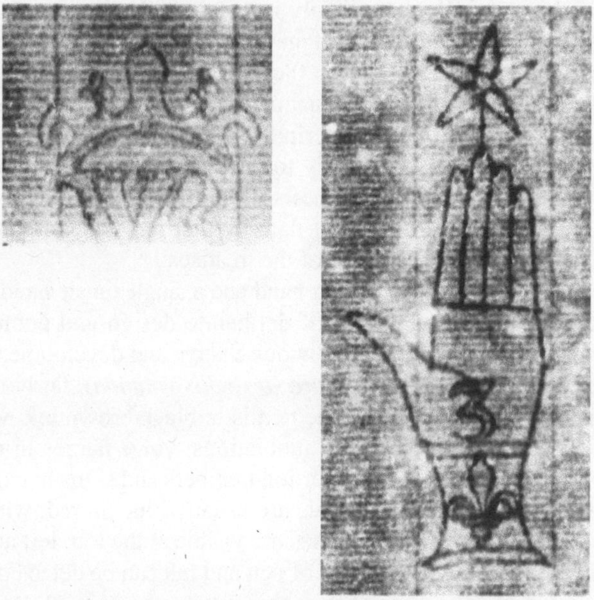

The watermark in the front flyleaf (figure 4a) demonstrates immediately that the flyleaves cannot be assumed to be original; the mark is a close match for Heawood's no. 1073 (London, 1725) and to a lesser extent nos. 1074–7, likewise dated in the 1720s.[138] The watermark on the back flyleaf, however, dates from the sixteenth century. The closest matches in Briquet, Piccard, and Heawood bear dates between 1539 and 1546; of these, the closest examples in Piccard and Heawood are from Canterbury and London and date between 1539 and 1541.[139] Whether or not the sheet was originally bound with the manuscript, the correspondence of possible dates and locations

[138]Edward Heawood, *Watermarks: Mainly of the 17th and 18th Centuries*, Monumenta chartæ papyraceæ historiam illustrantia, vol. 1 (Hilversum: Paper Publications Society, 1950; reprint, 1981), 88.

[139]The approximate matches (none is exact) are Briquet, no. 11370 (Dordrecht, 1545); Heawood, no. 2497 (Canterbury MSS, 1541) and possibly no. 2524 (State Papers, 1544–46); and Piccard, *Findbuch* 17, no. 1481 (London, 1539, 1540). C. M. Briquet, *Les Filigranes: Dictionnaire historique des marques du papier dès leur apparition vers 1282 jusqu'en 1600*, 4 vols. (Paris Picard; Geneva: Jullien, 1907), 4:574; Heawood, *Watermarks*, 119–20; Gerhard Piccard, *Die Wasserzeichenkartei Piccard im Hauptstaatsarchiv Stuttgart*, Findbuch 17, *Wasserzeichen: Hand und Handschuh* (Stuttgart: W. Kohlhammer, 1997), 33.

with our knowledge of John Dygon is remarkable and suggests that the sheet travelled with the book from an early period (perhaps as a cover). If the monk took up the name Wyldebore only in 1538, as the documents related to the dissolution of St. Augustine's suggest, then the temporal aspect of the authorial inscription on f. 12^{r} fits into the picture perfectly (see pp. 16–18 *supra*). By dating the copying of the manuscript to the period following the dissolution of St. Augustine's, the inscription agrees well with the dating of the watermark. The book is very likely to have been assembled, therefore, even as late as the 1540s. This hypothesis has little to contradict it, even if the style of notation was fairly out of date by then, nor does it rule out a much earlier date for the composition of the treatises.[140]

The appearance of only a single text hand and a single music hand in **GB-**Ctc O.3.38 confirms the impression of deliberate design and compilation over a short span of time; there is no obvious change and development of the hand. The text script is a rounded *textura* (*textualis rotunda*), fairly neat but not of professional quality. Most of the text is in black/brown ink, with red ink used for special marks: marginal annotations, voice names in musical examples, centered section titles, proportion numbers and signs in examples, and occasional capitals. Painted capitals are usually blue on red, with some cases in red only. Light brown guidelines are visible at the top, left and right margins of each written page. Changes of pen and ink can be detected at several points in the manuscript, notably at the juncture between the two treatises. The authorial inscription on f. 12^{r} was clearly written with a smaller pen nib than that used for the main text, although the hand appears to be the same. Similarly, comparison of the ink used in the music examples at the beginning of the second treatise (f. 13^{r}) and the end of the first treatise (f. 12^{r}) reveals a noticeable distinction in color, suggesting that the scribe did not continue immediately from one to the next.[141]

That the text scribe of **GB-**Ctc O.3.38 is very likely to have been the same person as the music scribe is suggested by the match of scribal hands between the proportion numbers (and signs) in the examples and in the text. The music hand, as noted (see p. 38 *supra*), makes use of certain specifically English notational features and in its use of colors displays all four styles current in early sixteenth-century England (black void, black full, red void, and red full). A notable characteristic of the manuscript is the layout of the musical examples within the text. For the majority of cases, particularly in

[140]See pp. 58–60 *supra*.

[141]Note, however, that examples of multiple black/brown inks appearing within single examples also occur at several points, particularly clearly on ff. 8^{r}–9^{r}.

the first treatise, the staves (which are straight but not rastrum-ruled) do not extend much farther than necessary to hold the music, rather than being ruled to a regular length. Text and music alternate in the manuscript with very little extra blank space, indicating that the scribe worked through the book sequentially rather than filling in text or music first, unless he was an extremely accurate judge of the space required by each.

The Edition

The readings of **GB**-Ctc O.3.38 form the basis for the present edition; they are sufficiently different from the source versions by Gaffurius to constitute a separate text. Except for the silent expansion of abbreviations and routine normalization of i/j and u/v, the edition retains Dygon's orthography, with its removal of Gaffurius's classicizing diphthongs and introduction of other "medieval" traits (such as -cio for -tio). All painted initials have been rendered as capitals; wherever a painted initial occurs, a new paragraph begins in the edition to preserve the visual distinction. In general, the frequent interruption of the text with musical examples and the consistent use of painted initials eliminate the need for further editorial division into paragraphs in the critical text, but in a few cases, extra paragraph divisions have been added to match the paragraphing in the translation. Punctuation in the edition mainly follows the manuscript, which is fairly systematic; conversion to modern punctuation conventions, in most cases, would effect no clarification of the grammatical structure (missing terminal punctuation has, however, been added). Errors in the text are fairly few and minor (although they occasionally point to misunderstandings of the text); these have been emended and are reported in the apparatus.

On the English translation pages, musical examples have been transcribed into a diplomatic score format that attempts to retain most of the features of the original notation. Ligatures are expanded into bracketed groups of separate notes. In both the unscored and scored examples, red coloration is indicated with angle brackets (⸢ and ⸣). Manuscript line endings are shown in the scored examples by a vertical dashed line; *custodes*, which are always shown correctly in the source, are therefore not recorded, along with clefs at new line beginnings (except where a change of clef occurs). Vertical and horizontal positioning of dots, sharps, and flats follows the source as closely as possible, although the original significance of horizontal positioning in particular is sometimes lost in the spacing required by score alignment. Editorial mensuration ticks have been added at the level of the brevis in the scored transcriptions.

The translation endeavors to present a clear English version of the manuscript text, while following the structure of the source as closely as possible. The treatises deal largely with practical and mathematical issues in a systematic way and therefore employ numerous technical terms, rendered as consistently as feasible in English. The major exception is in the naming of specific proportions and *genera*, which are left in Latin. English numerical nomenclature still tends to draw heavily on the Latinate terminology from which it is derived: the distinction between words such as "quadruple" and "quadrupla," or "septuple" and "septupla," make little difference for the reader's comprehension. More important, however, the need for single, contained terms to name proportions causes particular difficulty in the more complex compound proportions, where the grammatical implications of the Latin names cannot be translated except through unwieldy English phrases. Rendering a term like *superbipartiens quintas* as "Superbipartient fifths"[142] is not only of minimal help for understanding but is also misleading: the Latin term, in which *quintas* is the object of *superbipartiens*, is transformed to imply that *quintas* is the main term, modified adjectivally by *superbipartiens*. Accuracy in the English translation of the entire term would come only at the expense of losing its viability as a single technical term. Similarly, names of proportions of the *genus superparticulare*, such as *sesquialtera*, have no simple English versions, and the reader will find them in other discussions of proportion in their Latin forms.[143]

---

[142] As in Irwin Young's translation: *The "Practica musicae" of Franchinus Gafurius* (Madison: University of Wisconsin Press, 1969), 215–16.

[143] This is the approach adopted by Clement Miller in his edition and translation of Franchinus Gaffurius, *Practica Musicae*, Musicological Studies and Documents, no. 20 (n.p.: American Institute of Musicology, 1968). It is also used in English treatises of the fifteenth and sixteenth centuries. Early writers clearly recognized the problematic aspects of translating technical proportional terms into English, and embraced the habit of leaving proportion names in Latin: "for as moche as þ^{e} namys of hem [*sc.* proportions] be more conuenientli & compendiusli sette in latin þan in englissh þerfor þ^{e} namis of hem shal stonde stille in latin" (**GB**-Lbl Lansdowne 763, f. 117^{r}).

CONSPECTUS CODICIS ET NOTARUM

Manuscript

C Cambridge, Trinity College, O.3.38 (1st half of 16th century), **GB**-Ctc

Reference

G Gaffurius, Franchinus, *Practica musice* (Milan: Ioannes Petrus de Lomatio, 1496)

Notes

ante corr.	before correction	*quin.*	fifth
in marg.	in margin	*ras.*	erasure
lin.	line	*scripsi*	I have written
post	after	*sup.*	above
pr.	first	*tit.*	title

⟨ ⟩ enclose letters, words, and symbols added by the editor's conjecture

Library sigla

GB-Ccc	Cambridge, Corpus Christi College
GB-Cgc	Cambridge, Gonville and Caius College
GB-Cmc	Cambridge, Magdalene College
GB-Ctc	Cambridge, Trinity College
GB-Cu	Cambridge, University Library
GB-Lbl	London, British Library
GB-Llp	London, Lambeth Palace
GB-Lpro	London, Public Record Office
GB-Ob	Oxford, Bodleian Library
GB-WRec	Windsor, Eton College Library
GB-Ybi	York, Borthwick Institute of Historical Research
I-Bc	Bologna, Civico Museo Bibliografico Musicale
I-Rvat	Rome, Biblioteca Apostolica Vaticana
US-NYpm	New York, Pierpont Morgan Library

⟨JOANNIS DYGONI
PROPORTIONES PRACTICABILES SECUNDUM GAFFURIUM⟩

|| De Genere multiplici et eius speciebus. f. 1r

Multiplex genus est quum maior numerus comparatus et superpositus minori comprehendit ipsum intra se pluries precise. ut bis vel ter vel quater et deinceps quia si bis maior continet minorem dicitur proportio dupla ut .ii. ad .i. et .iiii. ad .ii. et .vi. ad .iii. hec enim prima species est multiplicis generis. in qua maior notularum numerus æquivalet minori. ita ut unaqueque

---

1–2 *scripsi* ||

JOHN DYGON
PRACTICAL PROPORTIONS ACCORDING TO GAFFURIUS

Concerning the *genus multiplex* and its species[1]

The *genus multiplex* is when a greater number, compared to and placed above a lesser number, includes a lesser number within itself several times exactly. For example: twice, thrice, four times, and so forth.[2] For if the greater contains the lesser twice, the proportion *dupla* is expressed. For example: two to one, four to two, and six to three. This is the first species of the *genus multiplex*, in which a greater number of notes equals a lesser

---

[1]The starting point of Dygon's treatise corresponds to Book IV, Chapter 3 of Gaffurius's *Practica musice.* In the absence of any type of introductory material (including even a title in the manuscript), the English treatises act to some extent as works of reference; the reader is assumed to have a working knowledge of mensural notation, which Gaffurius's audience would have encountered in the earlier books of the *Practica musice.* For a comparison of subjects treated in the books of Gaffurius and Dygon, see the Introduction, pp. 26–28 *supra.*

The set of proportions is divided into a number of *genera* to describe different types of ratios; each *genus* is divided into species, representing individual proportion types (see pp. 29–31 of the Introduction for a detailed explanation). Two further distinctions are lacking in Dygon's text: the differentiation between equal and unequal proportions; and the division of unequal proportions into proportions of greater and lesser inequality (both described in Book IV, Chapter 1 of the *Practica musice*).

[2]This basic definition of the *genus multiplex,* like all of the other genus definitions in the book, is standard and can be found (in variant forms) in countless writings on proportions (whether treating musical rhythms or not); e.g., Prosdocimo de' Beldomandi, *Brevis summula proportionum quantum ad musicam pertinent; Parvus tractatulus de modo monacordum dividendi,* ed. and trans. Jan Herlinger, Greek and Latin Music Theory, vol. 4 (Lincoln: University of Nebraska Press, 1987), 52–53. The definition in late sources such as the present work can probably be traced back originally in the West to Boethius's *De institutione musica* 1.4: "Est vero multiplex, ubi maior numerus minorem numerum habet in se totum vel bis vel ter vel quater ac deinceps [The multiple is where the greater number has in itself the whole lesser number either twice or three times or four times and so on]" (A. M. S. Boethius, *De institutione arithmetica libri duo, De institutione musica libri quinque,* ed. Godofredus Friedlein [Leipzig: B. G. Teubner, 1867], 191).

notula maioris dimidia sui quantitate minuatur: figuratur enim in cantibus hoc modo 2 ad 1. 4 ad 2. 6 ad 3. quod presentis concentus descriptione notatur.

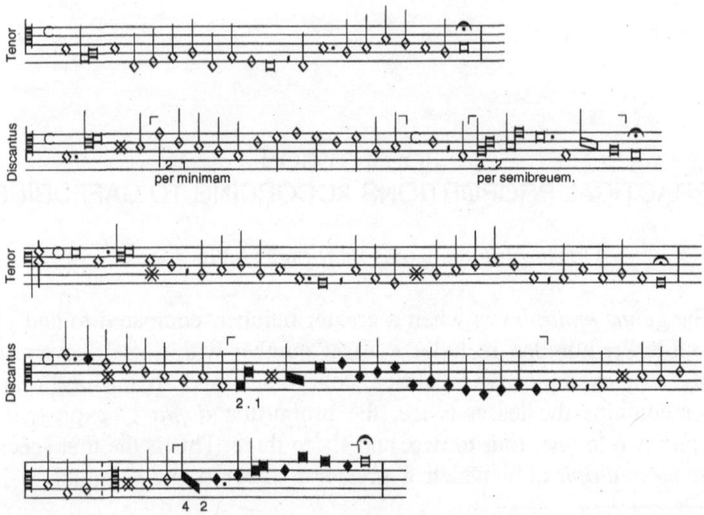

Hoc vero et semper memorie mandandum est ut due 𝅗𝅥 𝅗𝅥 ad unam 𝅗𝅥 et due ◊ ◊ ad unam semibrevem. Et si volueris due breves ad unam brevem. set raro aut nunquam per ⊟ esse videtur. Sic igitur hanc proportionem componere queas. ut superius notatur.

4–5 Dupla. *in marg.* C || 10 uolueris) due C ||

number, in such a way that every note of the greater number is diminished by half of its quantity. It is written out in songs in this way: 2 to 1; 4 to 2; 6 to 3. This is recorded in the notation of the present piece:[3]

However, one must always commit the following to memory: that two ♩ ♩ are compared to one ♩, and two ◊ ◊ to one semibrevis (and, if you wish, two breves to one brevis, but this proportion rarely or never seems to occur at the level of the ⊟).[4] In this way therefore (as recorded above) you can compose this proportion.

---

[3]The systematic illustration of the text with musical examples of this type is an idea Gaffurius found in Tinctoris's *Proportionale* and expanded. Among the earliest such theoretical examples demonstrating the rhythmic application of proportions with numerals are those in the (early fifteenth-century?) English treatise beginning *Pars aliquota est* (I-Rvat Reg. lat. 1146, ff. 48r–51r); although Prosdocimo's *Tractatus practice de musica mensurabili* describes the use of numerals for this purpose, no corresponding musical examples are provided (*Scriptorum de musica medii aevi nova series a Gerbertina altera*, 4 vols., ed. Edmond de Coussemaker [Paris: Durand, 1864–76; reprint, Hildesheim: Olms, 1963], 3:218). See also the Introduction, pp. 3–5 *supra*. That Dygon chose to replace Gaffurius's examples with his own, while retaining the basic format of the text, is demonstrative: while creating a substantial body of original musical material in his treatises, Dygon retained the elements of the *Practica musice* that could be considered the most generic.

[4]Here Dygon first expresses his concern for the rhythmic level at which a proportion occurs, an idea that Gaffurius does not treat. Dygon's examples carefully demonstrate proportions at the level of either the minima or semibrevis; the theorist later criticizes those

|| Secunda species. f. 1v

Tripla proportio est quum maior numerus continet minorem in se ter precise. ut .3. ad 1. 6 ad 2. 9 ad 3. in hac proportione tres notule equivalent uni sibi ipsis nomine et quantitate consimili. et hoc modo figuratur. 3.1.6.2. et ut hic declarat concentus.

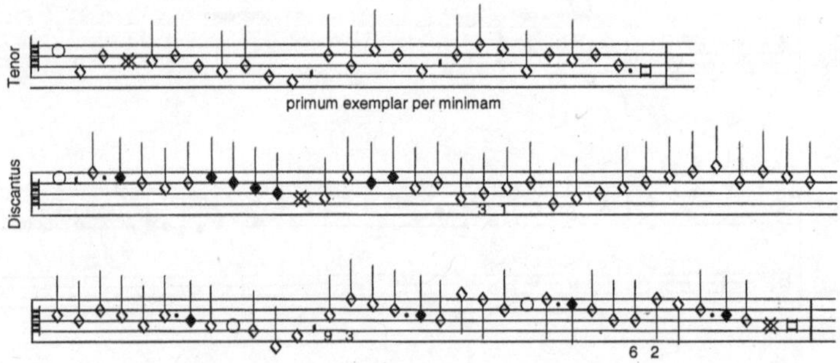

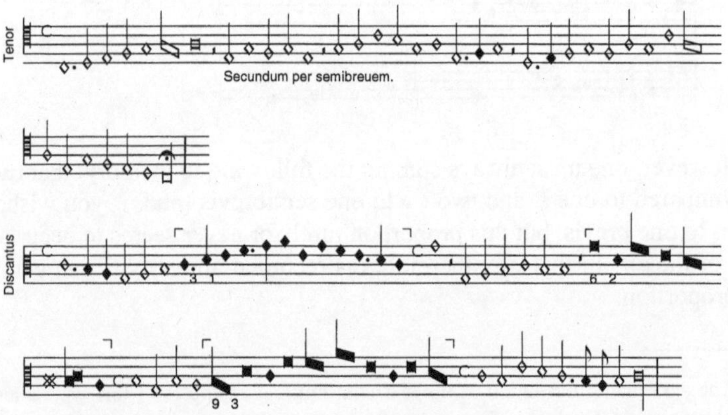

Quadrupla proportio fit cum maior numerus continet in se minorem quater precise. ut 4 ad 1. 8 ad 2. et 12 ad 3. et tercia multiplicis generis est. in hac etiam proportione quatuor semibreves uni semibrevi in quantitate et

---

2 quum]qum C || 6–8 Tripla .♩. *in marg.* C | *ras. post* per C || 9–12 Tripla .◊. *in marg.* C | 13 3.ª species *in marg.* C ||

Second Species

The proportion *tripla* is when a greater number contains a lesser number within itself exactly three times. For example: 3 to 1, 6 to 2, and 9 to 3. In this proportion, three notes equal one of the same name and quantity, and it is written out in this way: 3 1; 6 2; as this piece demonstrates:

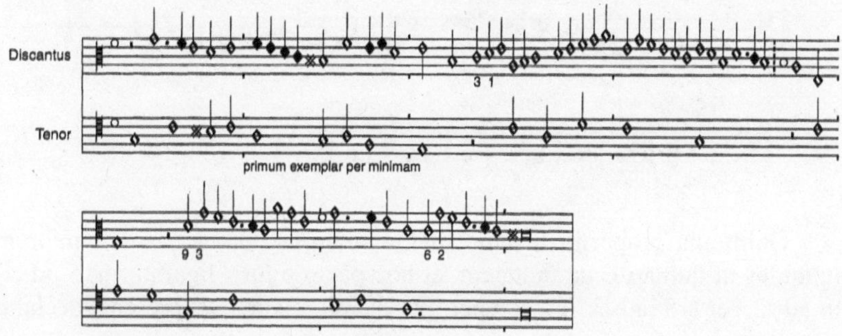

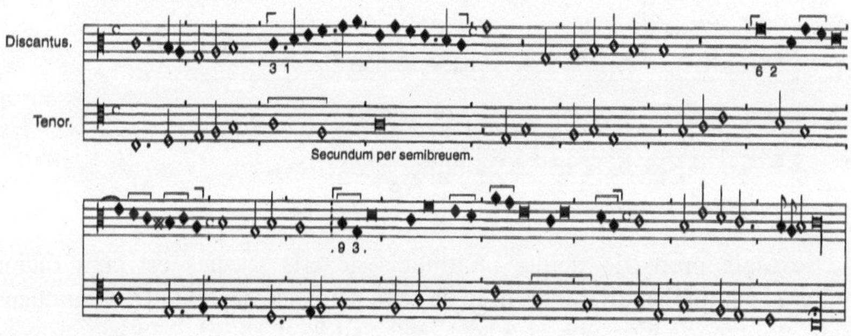

The proportion *quadrupla* occurs when a greater number contains a lesser number within itself exactly four times. For example: 4 to 1, 8 to 2, and 12 to 3; and it is the third species of the *genus multiplex*. In this proportion four semibreves are compared to and equal one semibrevis in quantity

---

who confuse levels by comparing minimae to semibreves (pp. 76–77 *infra*; see also Introduction, pp. 36 and 51).

mensura comparantur et equivalent. ita ut singula queque ipsarum quatuor minuatur de tribus quartis partibus sui quantitativi valoris. ut hic notatur.

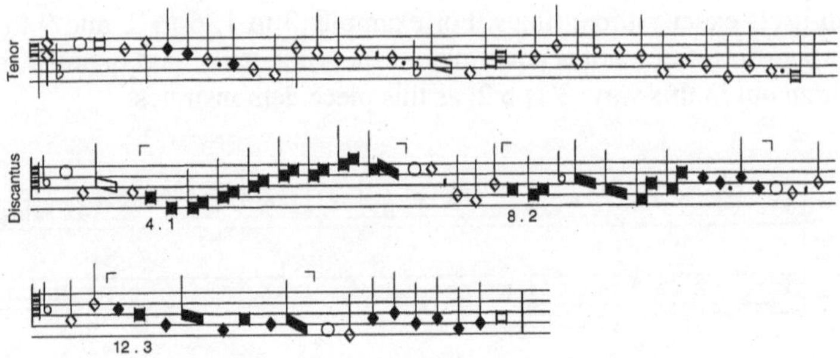

|| Quintupla proportio fit cum maior numerus continet in se minorem f. 2r
quinquies ut quinarius ad unitatem. et hoc pacto figuris figuratur ut 5 ad .1. 10 ad 2. et 15 ad 3. et semper per semibrevem. ut presens declarat concentus.

Sextupla proportio quinta multiplicis generis species est cum maior numerus comprehendit minorem in se sexies precise et equivalet ei in quantitate et temporis mensura. ut 6 ad 1. et 12 ad 2. et 18. ad 3. In hac propor-

6 4.ª species *in marg.* C | 7 quinquies]quinque C | 12 5.ª species *in marg.* C ||

and measure, so that every one of the four is diminished by three quarters of its quantitative value, as is recorded here:

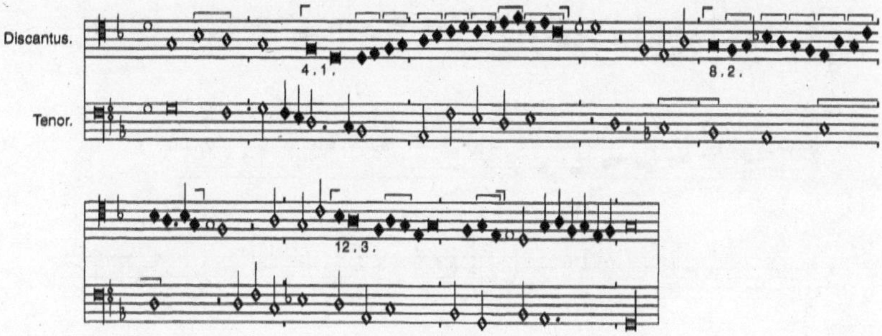

The proportion *quintupla* occurs when a greater number contains a lesser number within itself five times. For example: 5 to 1. It is written out with figures in this way: 5 to 1, 10 to 2, and 15 to 3; and it always occurs at the level of the semibrevis, as the following piece demonstrates:

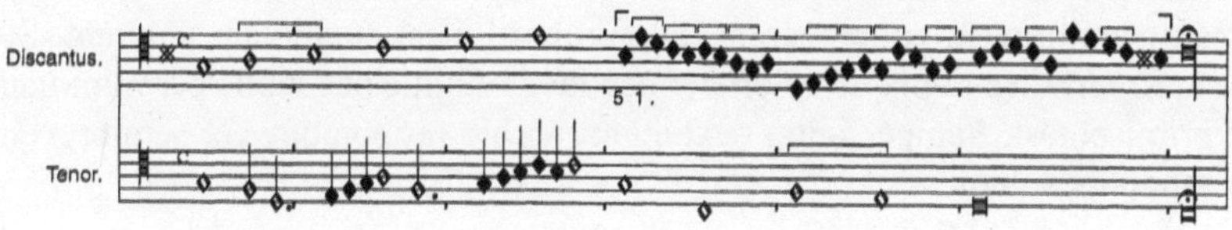

The proportion *sextupla*, the fifth species of the *genus multiplex*, is when a greater number includes a lesser number within itself exactly six times and equals it in quantity and measure of time. For example: 6 to 1, 12 to 2, and 18 to 3. In this proportion six semibreves are made commensurate with one

tione sex semibreves uni scilicet semibrevi nomine et quantitate commensurantur. ut in hoc notularum ordine notissime disponitur.

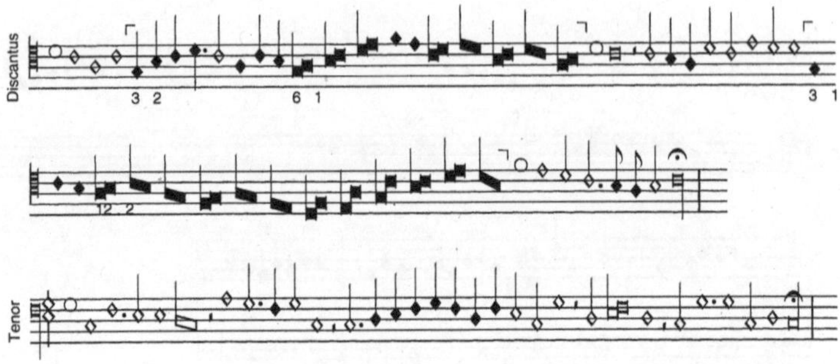

Huic vero proportioni sextuple due, ut vides, inductiones sunt. prima sesqualtera. secunda tripla. quibus facile et vere hanc proportionem sextuplam mensurare queas. Multi vero et, ut dicam, indocti proportionem triplam pro sextupla componunt. sex enim minimas ad unam semibrevem imponunt. quod est tripla. Si sex minimas ad unam minimam. aut sex semibreves ad unam semibrevem componerent tunc proportionem sextuplam viderent. Set hec proportio sextupla ob celeritate nec facile digitis nec labiis per minimam exprimi potest. Semper igitur sextuplam, ut hic proponitur. per semibrevem componere solemus.

semibrevis in name and quantity, as is set most notably in this arrangement of notes:

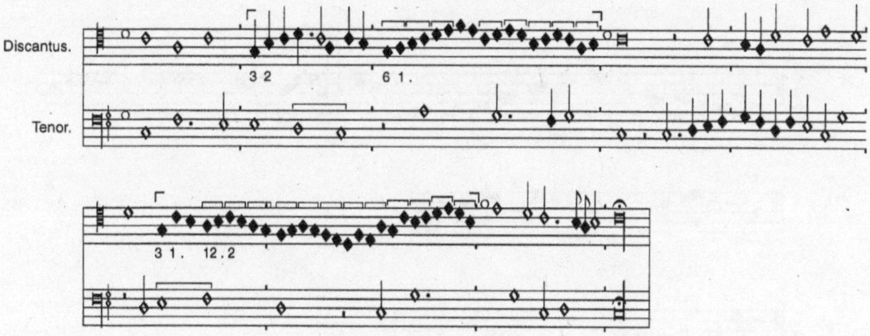

However, this proportion *sextupla* has two *inductiones*, as you see.[5] The first is *sesquialtera*, and the second is *tripla*. With these *inductiones* you can measure this proportion *sextupla* easily and truly. Many, however (and I would say, unlearned), compose in the proportion *tripla* in place of *sextupla*; for they set six minimae against one semibrevis, which is *tripla*. If they were to compose six minimae to one minima, or six semibreves to one semibrevis, then they would see the proportion *sextupla*. But on account of its swiftness, this proportion *sextupla* cannot be executed easily at the level of the minima, neither by fingers nor by lips; therefore we are accustomed always to compose the proportion *sextupla* at the level of the semibrevis, as is proposed here.

[5]This entire paragraph represents an interjection by Dygon into Gaffurius's structure, explaining the British practice of using *inductiones*: employing a common proportion to lead into an uncommon or difficult proportion. See the Introduction, pp. 34–36 *supra*.

Septupla proportio fit cum maior numerus continet minorem septies precise equivalens ipsi in quantitate et mensura. ut 7 ad 1 et 14 ad 2. septem semibreves uni semibrevi commensuratur. ut hic patet.

|| Octupla proportio fit cum maior numerus comprehendit minorem octies in se precise equivalens ei in potencia et mensura et septima speties multiplicis generis est. Hec proportio octo semibreves uni scilicet semibrevi equifacit. ut in hoc notularum ordine demonstratur. et hoc modo figuratur. ut 8 ad 1 et 16 ad 2 et 24 ad 3. f. 2v

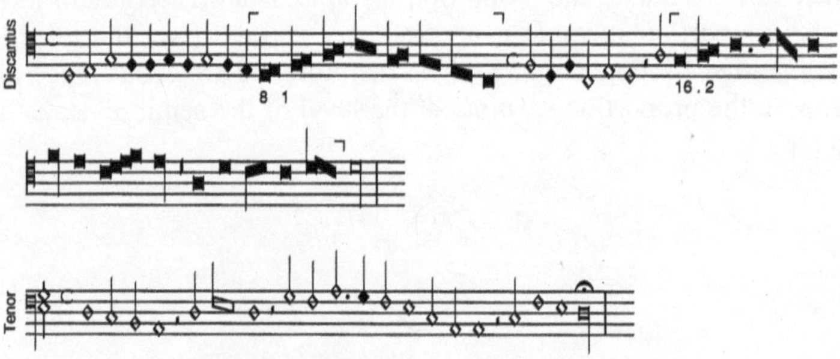

Satis tractatum de genere multiplici.

The proportion *septupla* occurs when a greater number contains a lesser number exactly seven times, equaling the lesser in quantity and measure. For example: 7 to 1 and 14 to 2. Seven semibreves are made commensurate with one semibrevis, as is shown here:

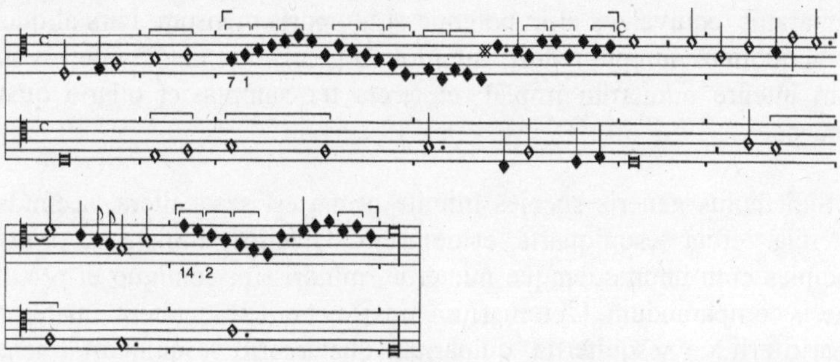

The proportion *octupla* occurs when a greater number includes a lesser number within itself exactly eight times, equaling the lesser in effect and measure; this is the seventh species of the *genus multiplex*. This proportion makes eight semibreves equal to one semibrevis, as is represented in this arrangement of notes; and it is written out in this way: 8 to 1, 16 to 2, and 24 to 3.

Enough concerning the *genus multiplex*.

⟨D⟩E genere superparticulari et eius speciebus.

Superparticulare genus quod secundum est maioris inequalitatis dicitur quum maior sequentium notularum numerus ad minorem precedentium quem semel tantum cum aliquota ipsius parte comprehendit noscitur esse comparatus. equivalens ei in potentia et temporis mensura. Pars aliquota est que aliquotiens sumpta reddit suum totum precise. ut media que bis sumpta suum integre numerum implet. et tercia ter sumpta. et quarta quater et deinceps.

Sunt huius generis species infinite prima est sesqualtera. secunda sesquitercia. tercia sesquiquarta. et deinceps. Quarum ordinem ac processum concipies cum unumquemque numerum minori sibi contiguo et proximiori duxeris comparandum. Ut ternarium binario et erit sesqualtera. quaternarium ternario eritque sesquitertia. quinarium quaternario sesquiquarta. senarium quinario sesquiquinta. et relique eodem modo.

Sesqualtera proportio fit cum maior numerus continet minorem semel tantum et insuper dimidiam ipsius partem equivalens ei in quantitate et mensura. ut 3. ad 2. et 6 ad 4. et 9 ad 6. In hac proportione tres minime ad duas minimas commensurantur. Item 3 semibreves ad duas semibreves simili modo ut hoc percipere facile possis concentu.

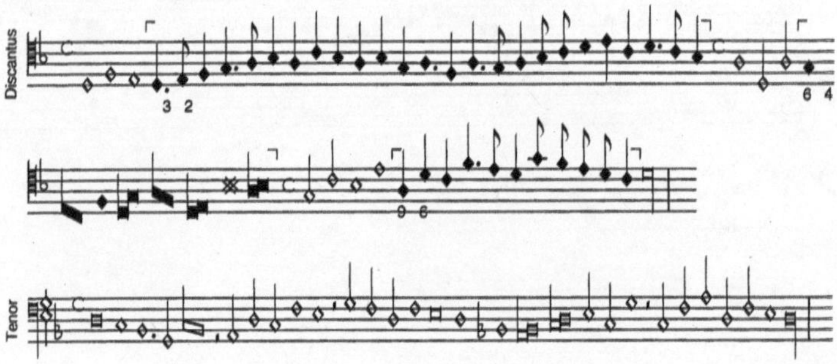

1 *scripsi* || 16 dimidiam]dimidium C || 18 semibreves (*pr.*)]semi *supra lin.* C ||

Concerning the *genus superparticulare* and its species

The *genus superparticulare*, which is the second *genus* of greater inequality,[6] is expressed when a greater number of following notes is compared to a lesser number of preceding notes, and the greater number, equaling the lesser in effect and measure of time, includes the lesser only once along with one of its aliquot parts. An aliquot part is a part that, when counted a certain number of times, makes up its whole exactly (for example: a half, which, when counted twice, fills its number completely; a third counted three times; a fourth four times; and so forth).[7]

The species of this *genus* are infinite. The first is *sesquialtera*, the second *sesquitertia*, the third *sesquiquarta*, and so forth. You will understand their arrangement and succession when you set up a comparison between any number and the contiguous and proximate smallest number. For example: a ternary number to a binary, which is *sesquialtera*; a quaternary to a ternary, which is *sesquitertia*; a quinary to a quaternary, *sesquiquarta*; a senary to a quinary, *sesquiquinta*; and the rest in the same way.

The proportion *sesquialtera* occurs when a greater number contains a lesser number only once, as well as half of the lesser, equaling the lesser in quantity and measure. For example: 3 to 2, 6 to 4, and 9 to 6. In this proportion three minimae are made commensurate to two minimae; likewise, three semibreves to two semibreves, as you can perceive easily in this piece:

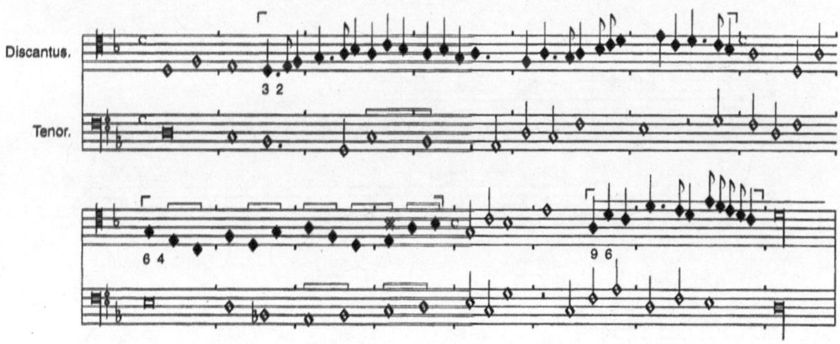

[6]Recall that Dygon, in skipping the first chapters of Book IV of the *Practica musice*, did not include an explanation of the *genera* of greater and lesser inequality. These terms refer to proportions in which the first number is greater or lesser than the second, respectively; Dygon only includes the *genera* of greater inequality in his treatises. See the Introduction, pp. 30–32 *supra.*

[7]An "aliquot part," in modern mathematical terminology, is a factor.

|| Sesquitercia proportio fit cum maior numerus continet minorem semel et insuper ipsius terciam partem. ut 4 ad 3. et 8 ad 6. et 12 ad 9. In hac autem proportione quatuor minime ad tres minimas commensurantur. ut hic probat concentus. f. 3r

Sesquiquarta proportio fit cum maior numerus continet minorem semel et insuper eius quartam partem. ut 5 ad 4. et 10 ad 8. et in hac proportione quinque minime ad quatuor minimas commensurantur. ut in notulis hic notatur.

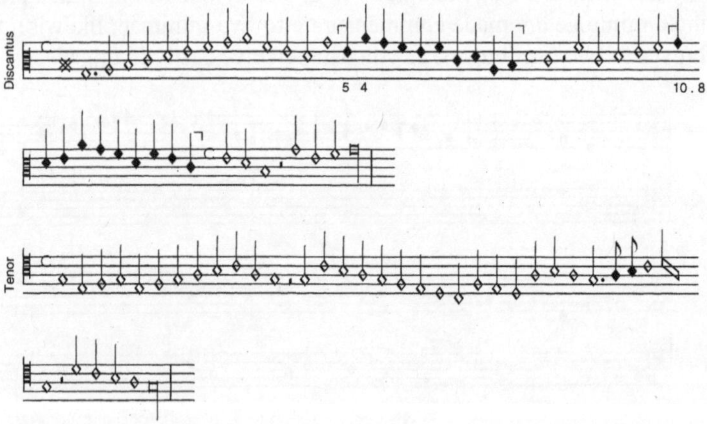

The proportion *sesquitertia* occurs when a greater number contains a lesser number once, as well as one third of the lesser. For example: 4 to 3, 8 to 6, and 12 to 9. Moreover, in this proportion four minimae are made commensurate to three minimae, as this piece verifies:

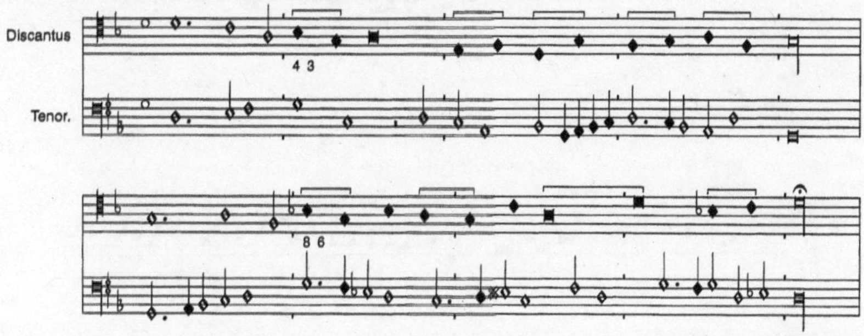

The proportion *sesquiquarta* occurs when a greater number contains a lesser number once, as well as one fourth of the lesser. For example: 5 to 4 and 10 to 8. In this proportion five minimae are made commensurate to four minimae, as is recorded in the notes here:

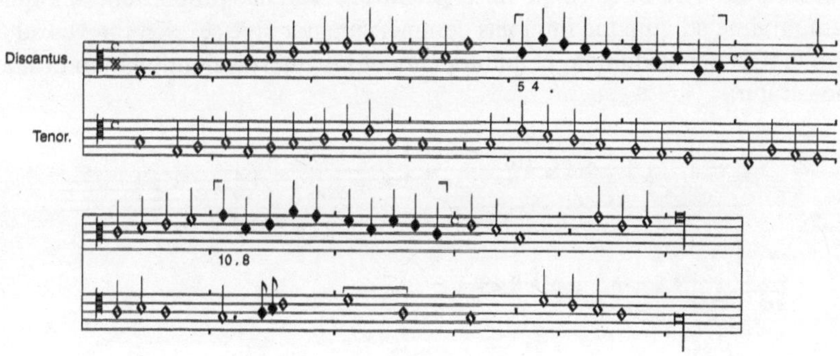

Hic quinque semibreves ad quatuor eis consimiles commensurantur. et per genus multiplicem.

|| Sesquiquinta proportio fit cum maior numerus comprehendit minorem semel et insuper eius minoris quintam partem equivalens ei in potentia et mensura. ut 6. ad 5. et 12 ad 10. et 18 ad 15. et in hac proportione sex quidem minime ad quinque minimas commensurantur sive sex semibreves ad 5 semibreves per sextuplam et quintuplam. ut hic inferius in notularum ordine monstratur. f. 3v

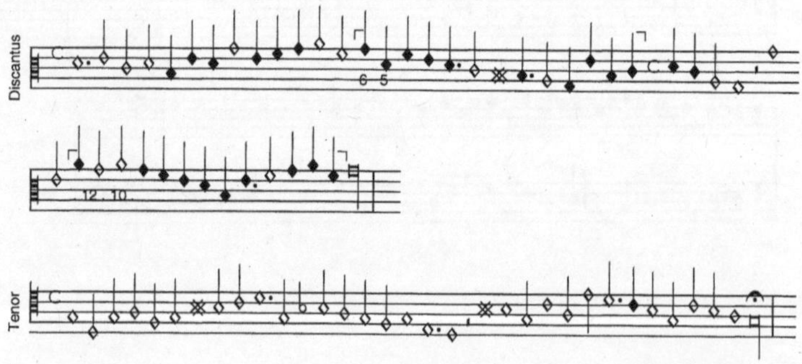

---

14 m. 8: ◆◊◊◆]◆◆◆◆C ||

Here five semibreves are made commensurate to four similar semibreves, through the *genus multiplex*:[8]

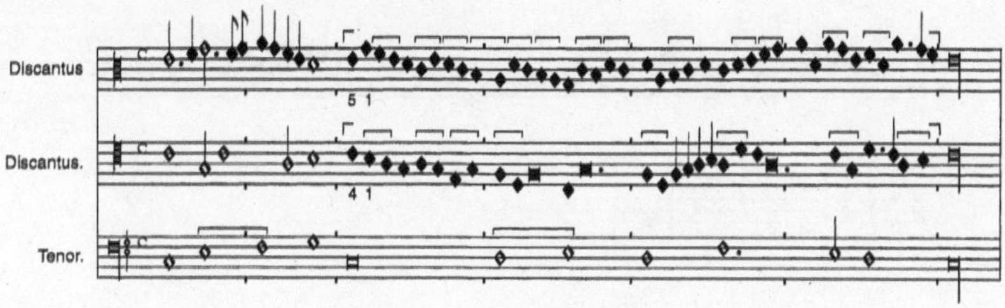

The proportion *sesquiquinta* occurs when a greater number includes a lesser number once, as well as one fifth of the lesser, equaling the lesser in effect and measure. For example: 6 to 5, 12 to 10, and 18 to 15. In this proportion six minimae are made commensurate to five minimae, or else six semibreves to five semibreves through *sextupla* and *quintupla*, as is presented in the arrangement of notes here below:

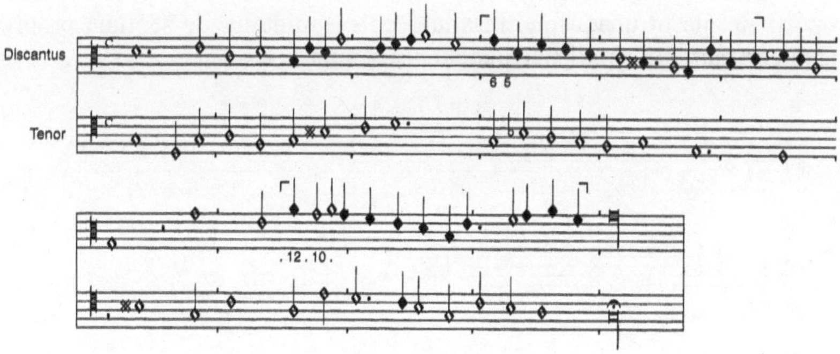

[8]This type of proportional demonstration, of which Dygon includes seven examples in total, is not present in Gaffurius's treatise. The process works by combining two simple proportions (in this case *quintupla* and *quadrupla*, both of the *genus multiplex*) to form a third proportion. Although a brief instance occurs in one of Dygon's motets, this type of proportional combination is extremely rare in practical usage. See the Introduction, pp. 43–44 *supra*.

Hic per sextuplam et quintuplam ut superius in canone dicitur. et Sesquiquinta proportio est.

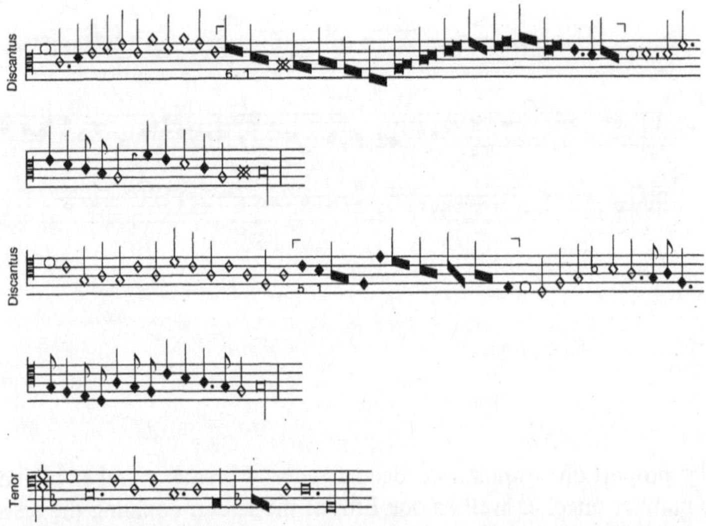

Sesquisexta proportio fit cum maior sequentium notularum numerus minori precedentium comparatus comprehendit ipsum semel et insuper sextam eius partem atque equatur ipsi in temporis mensura. ut 7 ad 6. et 14 ad 12. et 21 ad 18. Septem enim notule equivalent sex sibi consimilibus in hac proportione. ita ut unaqueque ipsarum septem minuitur de septima proprie quantitatis parte. In cantilenis quidem describitur hoc modo.

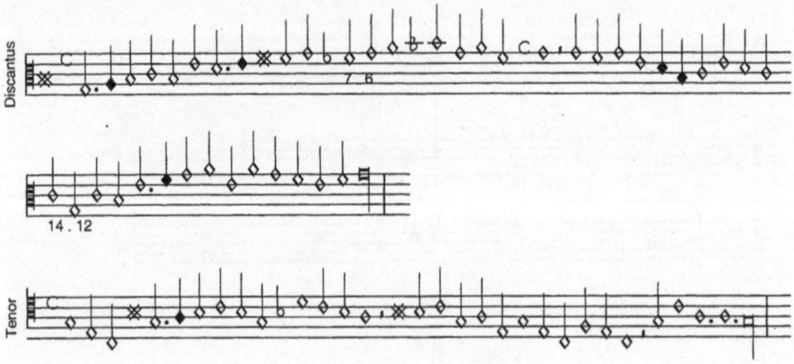

---

9 minori]minor C || 12 unaqueque]unaquaque C ||

Here the proportion *sesquiquinta* is formed through *sextupla* and *quintupla*, as expressed in the rule above.[9]

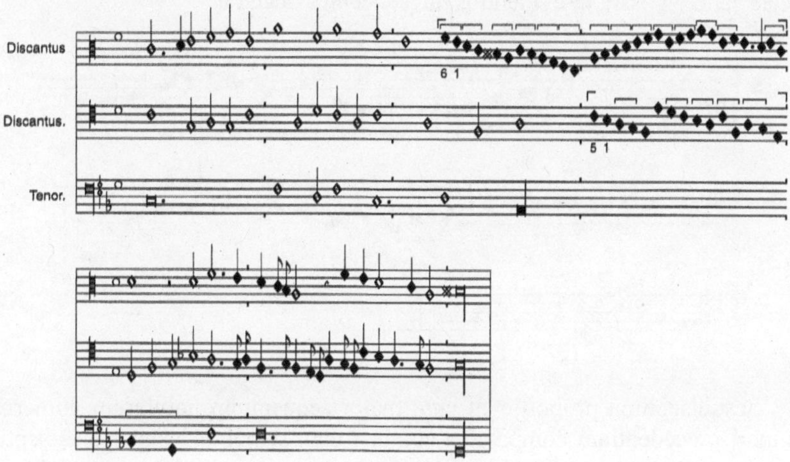

The proportion *sesquisexta* occurs when a greater number of following notes, compared to a lesser number of preceding notes, includes the lesser number once, as well as one sixth of the lesser; and it is equated with the lesser in measure of time. For example: 7 to 6, 14 to 12, and 21 to 18. For in this proportion seven notes equal six similar notes, in such a way that every one of those seven notes is diminished by a seventh of its own quantity. In songs it is notated in this way:

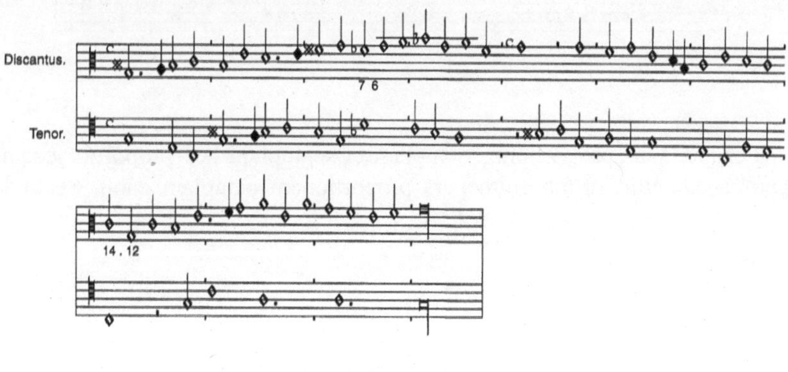

---

[9]I.e., in the second paragraph concerning *sesquiquarta* (see n. 8 *supra*).

|| Et hanc proportionem sesquisextam per genus multiplicem hoc est per proportionem septuplam ad sextuplam canere quimus, si quis septuplam recte canere possit, ut evidentius hic concentus declarat. f. 4r

Sesquiseptima proportio fit cum maior sequentium notularum numerus minori precedentium comparatus continet eum semel et insuper eius septimam partem equivalens ipsi in potencia et mensura. ut 8 ad 7. et 16 ad 14. et 24 ad 21. ut hic notatur.

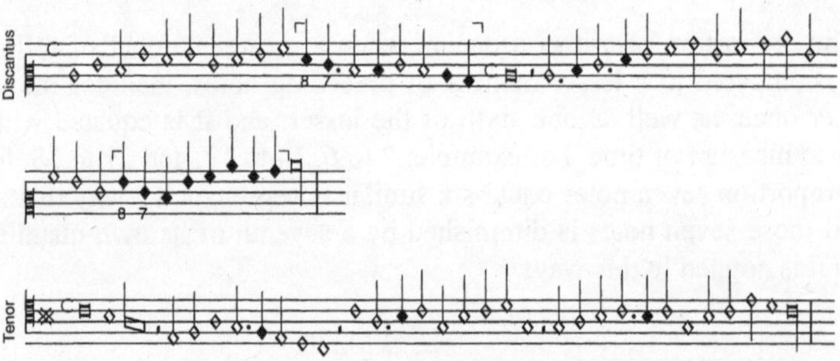

Per has duas proportiones octuplam et septuplam hec proportio sesquiseptima cantetur. prima enim pars proportionem octuplam canit. Secunda

We can also sing this proportion *sesquisexta* through the *genus multiplex*, that is, through the proportion *septupla* against *sextupla*—if anyone can sing *septupla* correctly—as this piece demonstrates clearly:[10]

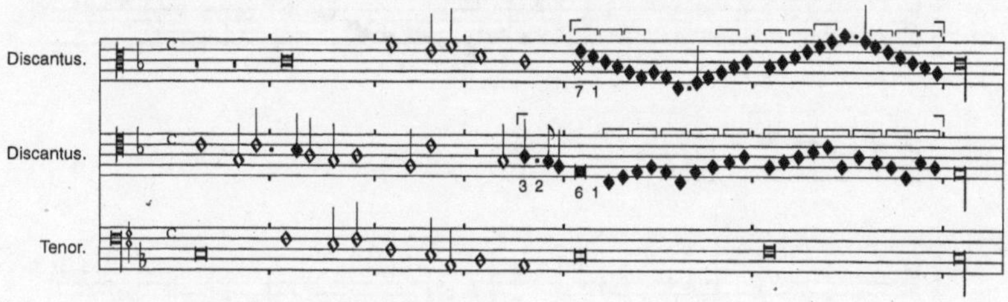

The proportion *sesquiseptima* occurs when a greater number of following notes, compared to a lesser number of preceding notes, contains the lesser number once, as well as one seventh of the lesser, equaling the lesser in effect and measure. For example: 8 to 7, 16 to 14, and 24 to 21, as is recorded here:

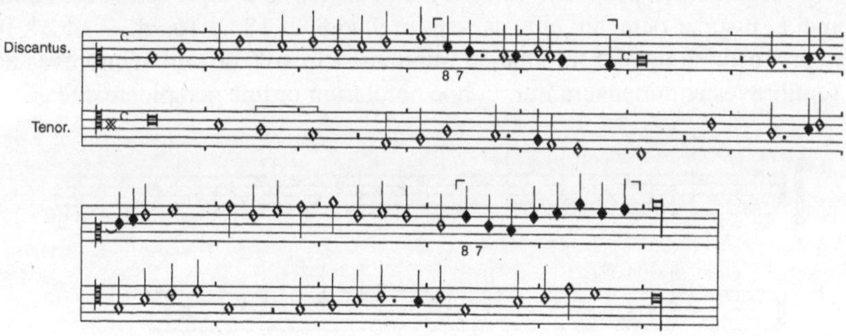

Let this proportion *sesquiseptima* be performed through these two proportions: *octupla* and *septupla*. For the first part sings the proportion *octu-*

---

[10]The brief passage of *sesquialtera* (3:2) in this example preceding *sextupla* (6:1) is a use of one of the *inductiones* mentioned by Dygon in his description of *sexta*; see pp. 76–77 *supra*.

septuplam. Sic inter has duas partes hic consequentes Sesquiseptima continetur.

|| Sesquioctava proportio fit cum maior numerus comprehendit minorem semel et insuper octavam eius partem. ut 9 ad 8. et 18 ad 16. et 27 ad 24. In hac proportione novem minime ad minimas octo sive novem semibreves ad 8 semibreves commensurantur. ut hoc notularum ordine perspicere queas. f. 4v

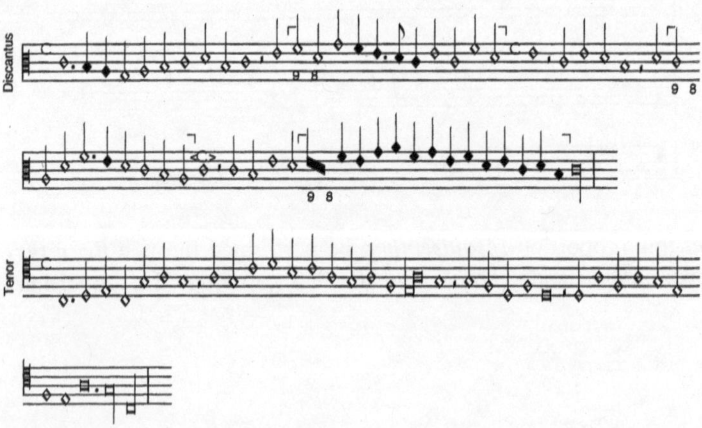

1–2 continetur.]continetur. ut hic. C || 6 m. 8: ♦♦■·♦♦■] ♦♦■♦♦■ C || 13 *scripsi* ||

pla, and the second, *septupla*. Thus *sesquiseptima* is contained between these two parts here following:

The proportion *sesquioctava* occurs when a greater number contains a lesser number once, as well as one eighth of the lesser. For example: 9 to 8, 18 to 16, and 27 to 24. In this proportion nine minimae are made commensurate to eight minimae, or else nine semibreves to eight semibreves, as you can examine in this arrangement of notes:

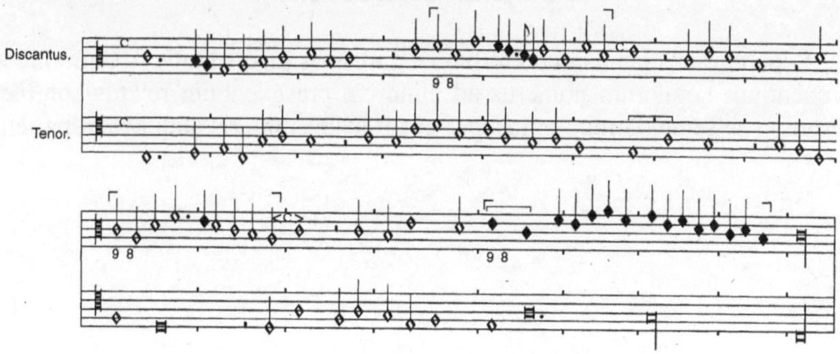

Hanc vero proportionem sesquioctavam per has duas proportiones quadruplamsesqualteram et quadruplam facilius, si diligentissime advertas, intelligere et canere possis. Prima enim pars in proportione quadruplasesqualtera, ut in cantilenis hic subpositis manifestissime notatur, habet novem semibreves ad duas semibreves. Secunda autem in quadrupla habet octo semibreves ad duas. Sic novem semibreves ad octo semibreves commensures velim. tum percipies quomodo hec proportio sesquioctava cantetur.

|| De genere superparcienti. f. 5r

Superpartiens genus quod tertium est maioris inequalitatis fit cum maior sequentium notularum numerus ad minorem precedentium relatus continet ipsum in se semel tantum et insuper unam ipsius minoris aliquantam partem

However, you can understand and sing this proportion *sesquioctava* more easily through these two proportions: *quadrupla sesquialtera* and *quadrupla*, if you ponder very carefully.[11] For the first part, in the proportion *quadrupla sesquialtera*, has nine semibreves to two semibreves, as is recorded very conspicuously in the cantilena here below. The second part, however, in *quadrupla*, has eight semibreves to two. In this way you should make nine semibreves commensurate to eight semibreves; then you will perceive how this proportion *sesquioctava* is performed.

Concerning the *genus superpartiens*

The *genus superpartiens*, which is the third *genus* of greater inequality, occurs when a greater number of following notes, in relation to a lesser number of preceding notes, contains a lesser number within itself only once, as well as an aliquant part drawn from several aliquot parts of the lesser

---

[11]Dygon perhaps forgets that *quadrupla sesquialtera* (9:2) has not yet been explained; it is probably used here rather than *nonupla* (9:1) because the latter would be too quick—recall Dygon's comments about *sextupla* at the level of the minima (pp. 76–77 *supra*) and note that the English book does not demonstrate any *multiplex* proportions beyond *octupla* (unlike Gaffurius's treatise). By using 9:2 here, comparing the proportions 9:2 and 8:2 will yield *sesquioctava* (9:8). In performance, the transition to 9:2 is aided by one of its *inductiones* in the example: after the passage of *sesquialtera* (3:2), the performer only need triple the pace to achieve *quadrupla sesquialtera* (9:2); see the Introduction, pp. 34–36.

ductam ex pluribus aliquotis. et ipse maior minori coequatur in potentia et temporis mensura.

Huius autem superpartientis generis infinite sunt species. Prima enim est Superbipartiens. Secunda supertripartiens. Tertia Superquatripartiens. Quarta Superquincupartiens. Quinta Supersexcupartiens. et sic ad infinita est processus. Prima species superbipartiens unum claudat inter terminos numerum. Secunda supertripartiens duos monstrat numeros inter terminos contineri. Tertia superquatripartiens tres numeros propriis intercipit terminis. Quarta superquincupartiens cuius termini quatuor intercipiunt numeros huiusmodi et relique in simpliciori et naturali numerorum dispositione procedunt.

Superbipartienstercias proportio fit quum maior sequentium notularum numerus ad minorem relatus continet eum semel et insuper unam aliquantam ipsius minoris partem ex duabus tertiis partibus factam et equivalet ipsi minori. ut v ad iii. et 10 ad 6. et 15 ad 9. In hac enim proportione quinque notule, sive minime sive semibreves sint, equivalent et commensurantur tribus sibi consimilibus. ut hoc probatur concentu.

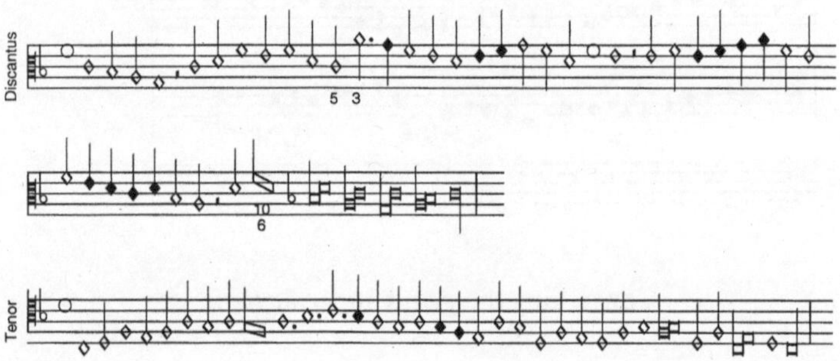

14 tertiis]tertius C ||

number.[12] The greater number is regarded as equivalent to the lesser in effect and measure of time.

The species of this *genus*, moreover, are infinite. The first is *superbipartiens*, the second *supertripartiens*, the third *superquatripartiens*, the fourth *superquincupartiens*, the fifth *supersexcupartiens*, and thus the succession continues to infinity. Let the first species, *superbipartiens*, enclose one number between its limits.[13] The second, *supertripartiens*, presents two numbers contained between its limits. The third, *superquatripartiens*, interposes three numbers between its own limits. The limits of the fourth, *superquincupartiens*, interpose four numbers of this kind; and the rest proceed in the very simple and natural disposition of numbers.

The proportion *superbipartiens tertias* occurs when a greater number of following notes, in relation to a lesser number, contains the lesser number once, as well as an aliquant part made of two thirds of the lesser.[14] The greater number equals the lesser. For example: 5 to 3, 10 to 6, and 15 to 9. In this proportion, five notes (whether they are minimae or semibreves) equal and are made commensurate with three similar notes, as is verified in this piece:

[12]An "aliquant part" of a number is a smaller number that is not one of its factors (e.g., 3, 5, 6, and 7 are aliquant parts of 8).

[13]I.e., one number is in between the first and second numbers of a *superbipartiens* proportion, so the difference between the numbers is 2 (e.g., 5:3, 7:5, and 9:7).

[14]On the naming convention for *superpartiens* proportions, see the Introduction, pp. 29–31.

Item hec quidem proportio Superbipartienstercias potest intelligi per has duas partes triplam quintuplamque canentes. ut quinarius ad ternarium numerum. ut hic.

|| Superbiparciensquintas proportio fit cum maior numerus comprehendit minorem semel et insuper duas ipsius minoris quintas partes. ut 7 ad 5. et 14 ad 10. et 21 ad 15. et septem semibreves equantur quinque sibi ⟨consimilibus⟩ et nomine et quantitate. ut hoc concentu facile consideratur. f. 5v

Superbipartiensseptimas proportio fit cum maior numerus continet minorem in se semel et insuper duas ipsius minoris septimas partes. ut 9 ad 7. et 18 ad 14. ut hic.

9 *scripsi* ||

Likewise, this proportion *superbipartiens tertias* can be understood through these two parts singing *tripla* and *quintupla*, as a quinary to a ternary number, as here:

The proportion *superbipartiens quintas* occurs when a greater number includes a lesser number once, as well as two fifths of the lesser number. For example: 7 to 5, 14 to 10, and 21 to 15. Seven semibreves are equated with five semibreves similar in name and quantity, as is easily considered in this piece:

The proportion *superbipartiens septimas* occurs when a greater number contains a lesser number within itself once, as well as two sevenths of the lesser number. For example: 9 to 7 and 18 to 14, as here:

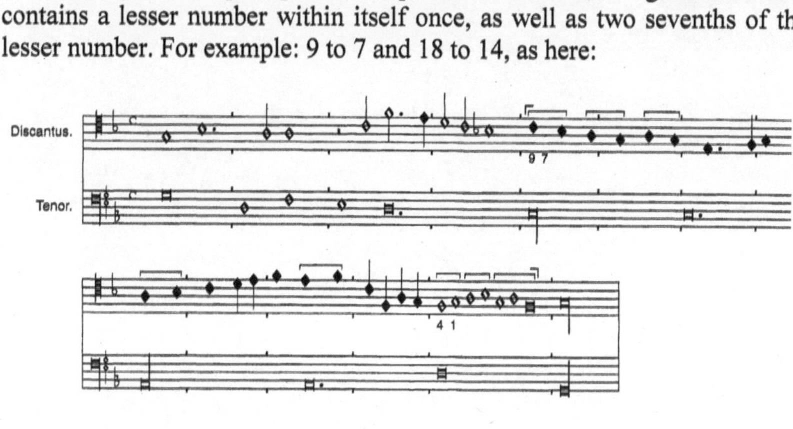

Supertripartiensquartas proportio fit cum maior numerus comprehendit minorem in se semel et insuper tres ipsius minoris quartas partes et equivalet ei in potencia et mensura. ut 7 ad 4. et 14 ad 8. et 21 ad 12.

Supertripartiensquintas proportio fit quum maior sequentium notularum numerus comparatus minori precedentium continet eum semel et insuper tres quintas ipsius minoris partes equivalens ei in potencia. ut 8 ad 5. et 16 ad 10. et 24 ad 15. et 8 semibreves ad 5 semibreves commensurantur. ut hic.

The proportion *supertripartiens quartas* occurs when a greater number includes a lesser number within itself once, as well as three fourths of the lesser number. The greater number equals the lesser in effect and measure. For example: 7 to 4, 14 to 8, and 21 to 12.

The proportion *supertripartiens quintas* occurs when a greater number of following notes, compared to a lesser number of preceding notes and equaling the lesser in effect, contains the lesser number once, as well as three fifths of the lesser number. For example: 8 to 5, 16 to 10, and 24 to 15. Eight semibreves are made commensurate to five semibreves, as here:

|| Supertripartiensseptimas proportio fit quum maior numerus continet minorem semel et insuper tres ipsius minoris septimas partes et equivalet ipsi minori. ut 10 ad 7 et 20 ad 14. et 30 ad 21. f. 6r

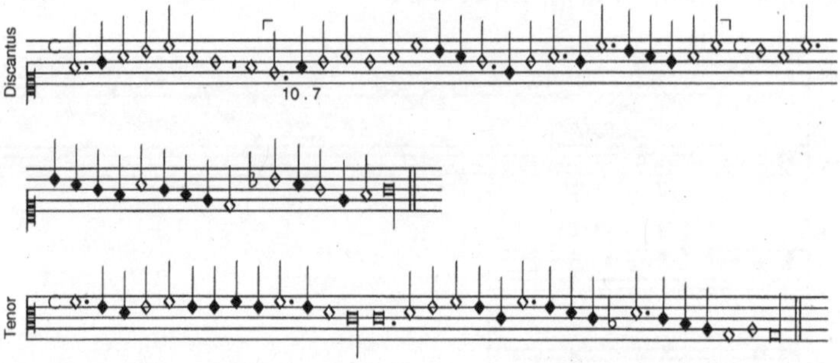

Superquatriparciensquintas proportio fit quum maior numerus comprehendit minorem in se semel et insuper quatuor quintas ipsius minoris partes et equivalet ipsi minori ut 9 ad 5. et 18. ad 10. et 27 ad 15. hec proportio novem semibreves ad quinque semibreves commensurat. ut hoc monstratur concentu.

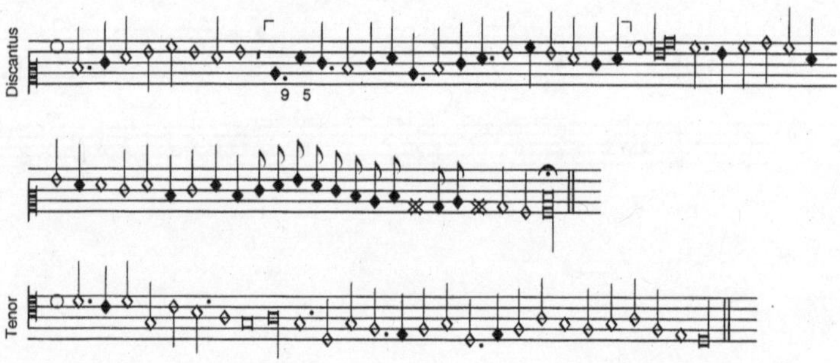

The proportion *supertripartiens septimas* occurs when a greater number contains a lesser number once, as well as three sevenths of the lesser number, and equals the lesser. For example: 10 to 7, 20 to 14, and 30 to 21.[15]

The proportion *superquatripartiens quintas* occurs when a greater number includes a lesser number within itself once, as well as four fifths of the lesser number, and equals the lesser number. For example: 9 to 5, 18 to 10, and 27 to 15. This proportion makes nine semibreves commensurate to five semibreves, as is presented in this piece:

[15]This example and the following one are the only two that Dygon copied from the *Practica musice*; for a comparison and discussion of their readings, see the Introduction, pp. 39–42.

Hec autem proportio Superquadripartiensquintas per has duas proportiones sequentes id est per quadruplamsesqualteram et duplamsesqualteram potest intelligi. ut presens declarat concentus.

|| Superquadripartiensseptimas proportio fit cum maior sequentium notularum numerus ad minorem precedentium relatus comprehendit et eum semel et insuper quatuor septimas ipsius minoris partes. ut 11 ad 7 et 22 ad 14. et 33 ad 21. In hac proportione undecim notule equivalent septem sibi f. 6v

2 quadruplamsesqualteram]quadruplamsequiquartam C ||

Also, this proportion *superquatripartiens quintas* can be understood through these two following proportions: *quadrupla sesquialtera* and *dupla sesquialtera*, as the present piece demonstrates:[16]

The proportion *superquatripartiens septimas* occurs when a greater number of following notes, in relation to a lesser number of preceding notes, includes the lesser number once, as well as four sevenths of the lesser number. For example: 11 to 7, 22 to 14, and 33 to 21. In this proportion eleven

[16]Once again, Dygon avoids the proportion *nonupla* (9:1) by using *quadrupla sesquialtera* (9:2); see n. 11 *supra*. As before, a proportion is used in this example that has not yet been explained (*dupla sesquialtera*, 5:2).

consimilibus. Ita ut unaqueque ipsarum undecim diminuatur de quatuor undenis partibus proprii valoris ut presens probat concentus.

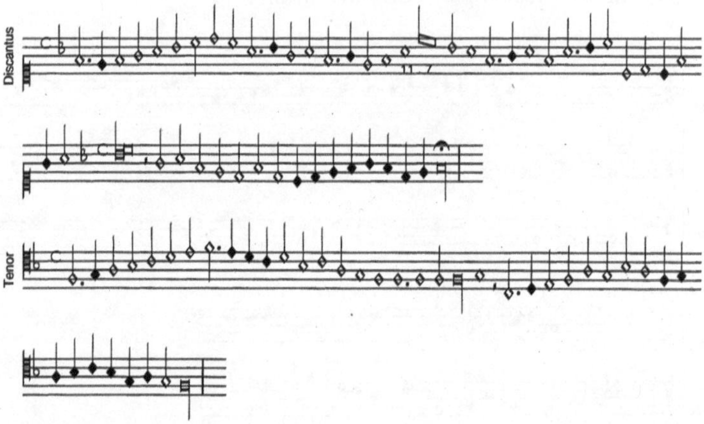

Superquatripartiensnonas proportio fit quum maior numerus comprehendit minorem in se semel et insuper quatuor ipsius partes nonas et coequatur ei in potentia et mensura. ut in notularum ordine et hic in figuris declaratur. ut 13 ad 9. et 26 ad 18. et 39 ad 27.

7 Superquatripartiensnonas]qua *sup. lin.* C || 12] C ||

notes equal seven similar notes, in such a way that every one of the eleven is diminished by four elevenths of its own value, as the present piece verifies:

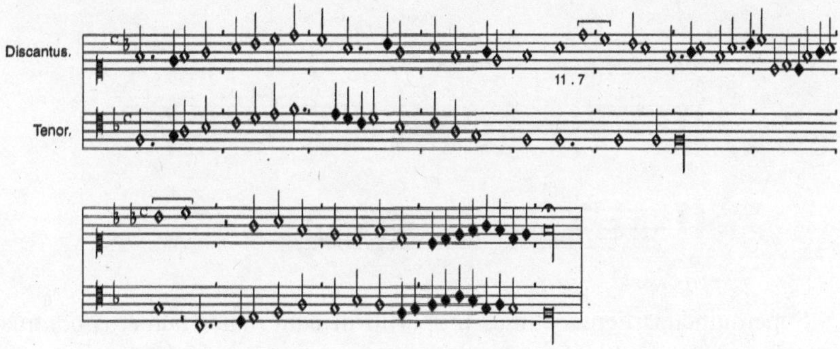

The proportion *superquatripartiens nonas* occurs when a greater number includes a lesser number within itself once, as well as four ninths of the lesser number, and is regarded as equivalent to the lesser in effect and measure, as is demonstrated in the arrangement of notes, and here with figures: 13 to 9, 26 to 18, and 39 to 27.

Superquincupartienssextas proportio fit quum maior numerus comprehendit minorem in se semel et insuper unam eius aliquantam partem ex quinque sextis partibus ipsius minoris. ut hic / 11 ad 6. et 22 ad 12. et 33 ad 18.

Superquincupartiensseptimas proportio fit cum maior numerus continet minorem in se semel et insuper quinque septimas ipsius minoris partes equivalens ⟨ei⟩ in potencia et mensura. ut 12 ad 7. et 24 ad 14.

|| Supersexcupartiensseptimas proportio fit quum maior numerus comprehendit minorem in se semel et insuper sex eius minoris septenas partes et coequatur ei in potencia. ut 13 ad 7 et 26 ad 14. f. 7r

Multiplexsuperparticulare genus quod quartum est maioris inequalitatis compositum ex duobus primis fit quum maior sequentium notularum numerus ad minorem precedentium relatus comprehendit eum pluries et insuper unam eius aliquotam partem.

---

9 *scripsi* ||

The proportion *superquincupartiens sextas* occurs when a greater number includes a lesser number within itself once, as well as one aliquant part made of five sixths of the lesser. For example: 11 to 6, 22 to 12, and 33 to 18.

The proportion *superquincupartiens septimas* occurs when a greater number contains a lesser number within itself once, as well as five sevenths of the lesser number, and equals the lesser in effect and measure. For example: 12 to 7 and 24 to 14.

The proportion *supersexcupartiens septimas* occurs when a greater number includes a lesser number within itself once, as well as six sevenths of the lesser number, and is regarded as equivalent to the lesser in effect. For example: 13 to 7 and 26 to 14.

The *genus multiplex superparticulare*, which is the fourth *genus* of greater inequality, composed of the first two *genera*, occurs when a greater number of following notes, in relation to a lesser number of preceding notes, includes the lesser multiple times, as well as one of its aliquot parts.

Huius autem generis infinite sunt species diversis gradibus considerande. Primus quidem gradus procedit ex prima multiplici singulis superparticularibus secundum naturalem earum dispositionem permixta. Ut duplasesqualtera. 5 ad 2. Duplasesquitertia 7 ad 3. Duplasesquiquarta 9 ad 4. Duplasesquiquinta. 11 ad 5. et deinceps.

Secundus gradus concipitur ex secunda multiplici omnium superparticularium naturaliter dispositarum susceptibili. ut Triplasesqualtera 7. 2. Triplasesquitercia. 10 ad 3. Triplasesquiquarta 13 ad 4. Triplasesquiquinta. 16 ad 5. et sic deinceps.

Tertius gradus omnes superparticularis generis habitudines tercie multiplici coniungit ut Quadruplasesqualtera. 9 ad 2. Quadruplasesquitercia. 13 ad 3. Quadruplasesquiquarta. 17 ad 4. Quadruplasesquiquinta. 21 ad 5. et deinceps.

In quarto gradu singule superparticulares quarte multiplici adherent. ut Quintuplasesqualtera. 11 ad 2. Quintuplasesquitertia. 16 ad 3. Quintuplasesquiquarta. 21 ad 4. Quintuplasesquiquinta. 26 ad 5. et deinceps. Atque ita infiniti sunt huius generis gradus. Graduumque species infinite.

Duplasesqualtera proportio fit quum maior numerus continet minorem bis et insuper dimidiam ipsius partem minorem equivalens ei in potentia et temporis mensura. ut 5 ad 2. et 10 ad 4. et 15 ad 6. In hac proportione quinque semibreves equivalent et commensurantur duabus semibrevibus. ut hic describitur.

2–3 superparticularibus]super particularibus C || 6–7 superparticularium]superparticularum C || 7 7. 2 *sup. lin.* C ||

The species of this *genus*, moreover, are infinite and must be considered in various degrees.[17] The first degree proceeds from the first *multiplex* species[18] mixed with the individual *superparticulare* species according to their natural disposition. For example: *dupla sesquialtera*, 5 to 2; *dupla sesquitertia*, 7 to 3; *dupla sesquiquarta*, 9 to 4; *dupla sesquiquinta*, 11 to 5; and so forth.

The second degree is devised from the second *multiplex* species taken together with all *superparticulare* species naturally disposed. For example: *tripla sesquialtera*, 7 to 2; *tripla sesquitertia*, 10 to 3; *tripla sesquiquarta*, 13 to 4; *tripla sesquiquinta*, 16 to 5; and so forth in this way.

The third degree joins all the attributes of the *genus superparticulare* to the third *multiplex* species. For example: *quadrupla sesquialtera*, 9 to 2; *quadrupla sesquitertia*, 13 to 3; *quadrupla sesquiquarta*, 17 to 4; *quadrupla sesquiquinta*, 21 to 5; and so forth.

In the fourth degree, the individual *superparticulare* species are attached to the fourth *multiplex* species. For example: *quintupla sesquialtera*, 11 to 2; *quintupla sesquitertia*, 16 to 3; *quintupla sesquiquarta*, 21 to 4; *quintupla sesquiquinta*, 26 to 5; and so forth. And thus the degrees of this *genus* are infinite, and the species of the degrees are infinite.

The proportion *dupla sesquialtera* occurs when a greater number contains a lesser number twice, as well as half of the lesser number, and equals the lesser in effect and measure of time. For example: 5 to 2, 10 to 4, and 15 to 6. In this proportion five semibreves equal and are made commensurate with two semibreves, as is notated here:

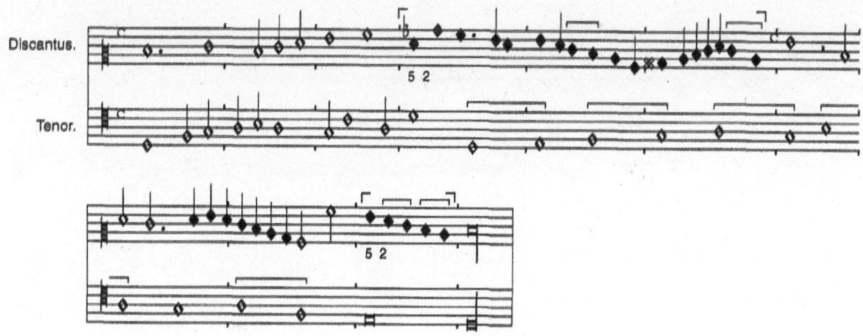

[17]For the *genera* that combine two *genera* together (*multiplex superparticulare* and *multiplex superpartiens*), an extra division into "degrees" comes between the level of *genus* and species. Each degree corresponds to one of the *multiplex* species; this degree is then divided into species corresponding to the species of *superparticulare* or *superpartiens*.

[18]I.e., *dupla*.

|| Duplasesquitertia proporcio fit quum maior numerus continet minorem bis et insuper terciam ipsius partem equivalens in potentia et mensura. ut 7 ad 3. 14 ad 6. 21 ad 9. f. 7v

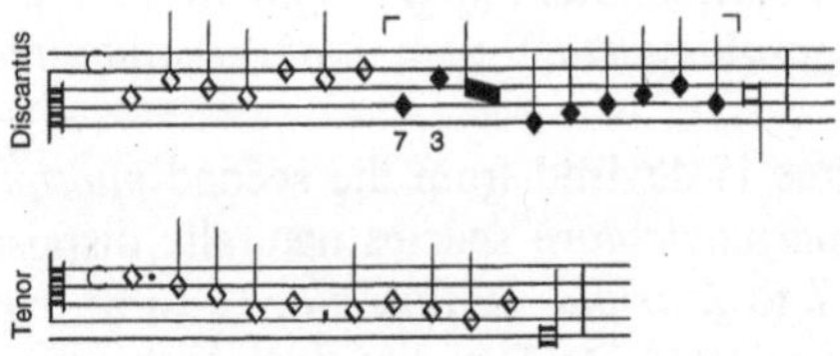

Duplasesquiquarta proportio fit cum maior numerus continet minorem bis et insuper quartam ipsius partem equivalens ei in potentia et temporis mensura. ut 9 ad 4. 18 ad 8. In hac proportione Duplasesquiquarta quo pacto in potencia et temporis mensura novem semibreves equivalere quatuor semibrevibus possint, sive nóvem minime quatuor minimis, hic in notularum ordine describitur.

4 m. 4 *pr. minima* G *ante corr.* C | *quint. minima* ♭ *ante corr.* C ||

The proportion *dupla sesquitertia* occurs when a greater number contains a lesser number twice, as well as a third of the lesser number. The greater number equals the lesser in effect and measure. For example: 7 to 3, 14 to 6, and 21 to 9.

The proportion *dupla sesquiquarta* occurs when a greater number contains a lesser number twice, as well as a fourth of the lesser number, and equals the lesser in effect and measure of time. For example: 9 to 4 and 18 to 8. The way in which, in this proportion *dupla sesquiquarta*, nine semibreves can equal four semibreves in effect and measure of time, or nine minimae four minimae, is notated in the arrangement of notes here:

Duplasesquiquinta proportio fit cum maior numerus comprehendit minorem bis et insuper quintam ipsius partem. ut 11 ad 5. et 22 ad 10. et 33 ad 15. Hec autem proportio undecim semibreves ad quinque semibreves, vel undecim minime ad quinque minimas sibi postulat. ut in cantilenis hic notatur.

|| Triplasesqualtera proportio fit cum maior numerus comprehendit mino- f. 8r
rem ter et insuper dimidiam eius partem. ut 7 ad 2. et 14 ad 4. et 21 ad 6. In hac proportione septem semibreves equivalent et commensurantur duabus semibrevibus. ita ut unaqueque ipsarum septem diminuatur de quinque septenis parcibus sue quantitatis. ut hic componitur.

The proportion *dupla sesquiquinta* occurs when a greater number includes a lesser number twice, as well as a fifth of the lesser number. For example: 11 to 5, 22 to 10, and 33 to 15. This proportion, moreover, requires eleven semibreves against five semibreves, or eleven minimae against five minimae, as is recorded in the cantilena here:

The proportion *tripla sesquialtera* occurs when a greater number includes a lesser number three times, as well as half of the lesser number. For example: 7 to 2, 14 to 4, and 21 to 6. In this proportion seven semibreves equal and are made commensurate with two semibreves, in such a way that each of the seven is diminished by five sevenths of its quantity, as is composed here:

Triplasesquitercia proportio fit cum maior numerus continet minorem ter et eius insuper terciam partem. ut 10 ad 3. et 20 ad 6. et 30 ad 9. Hec autem proportio decem semibreves tribus semibrevibus equat in temporis mensura quo singula queque ipsarum decem de septem decenis partibus sui valoris detrimentum patiatur. ut presens declarat concentus.

Triplasesquiquarta proportio fit cum maior numerus continet minorem ter et eius insuper quartam partem. ut 13 ad 4. et 26 ad 8. et 39 ad 12. In hac proportione tresdecim semibreves equivalent et commensurantur quatuor semibrevibus. ita ut unaqueque ipsarum tresdecim diminuatur de novem terdenis partibus proprie quantitatis. ut in his proporcionatur cantilenis.

---

4 singula]singule C || 11 commensurantur]commesurantur C ||

The proportion *tripla sesquitertia* occurs when a greater number contains a lesser number three times, as well as a third of the lesser number. For example: 10 to 3, 20 to 6, and 30 to 9. This proportion, moreover, equates ten semibreves with three semibreves in measure of time, so every one of the ten suffers the loss of seven tenths of its value, as the present piece demonstrates:

The proportion *tripla sesquiquarta* occurs when a greater number contains a lesser number three times, as well as a fourth of the lesser number. For example: 13 to 4, 26 to 8, and 39 to 12. In this proportion thirteen semibreves equal and are made commensurate with four semibreves, in such a way that each of the thirteen is diminished by nine thirteenths of its own quantity, as is proportioned in these cantilena:

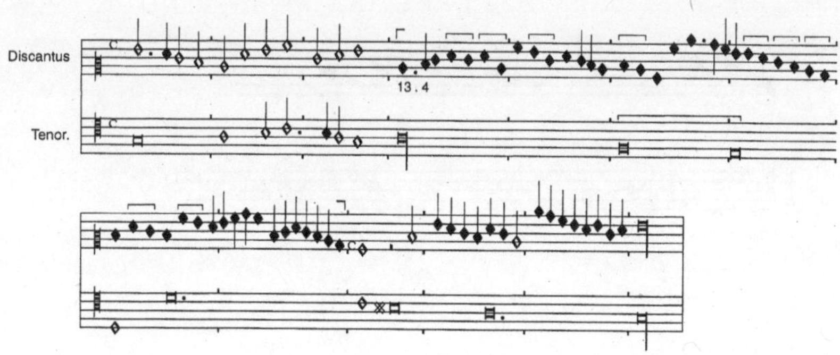

|| Quadruplasesqualtera proportio fit cum maior numerus comprehendit minorem quater et insuper dimidiam eius partem. ut 9 ad 2. et 18 ad 4. et 27 ad 6. Si hanc proportionem recte commensurare volueris, accipias velim has duas proportiones id est triplam et sesqualteram pro inductione. ut hic in cantilenis notatur. f. 8v

Quadruplasesquitertia proportio fit quum maior numerus comprehendit minorem quater et eius insuper .3. partem. ut 13 ad 3. et 26 ad 6. et 39 ad 9. In hac autem proportione tresdecim semibreves ad tres semibreves sunt. ut hic describitur.

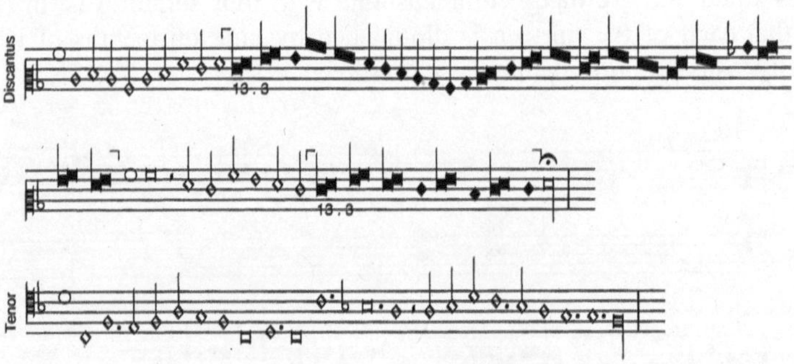

The proportion *quadrupla sesquialtera* occurs when a greater number includes a lesser number four times, as well as half of the lesser number. For example: 9 to 2, 18 to 4, and 27 to 6. If you would like to measure this proportion correctly, you should use as an *inductio* these two proportions: *tripla* and *sesquialtera*, as is recorded in the cantilena here:[19]

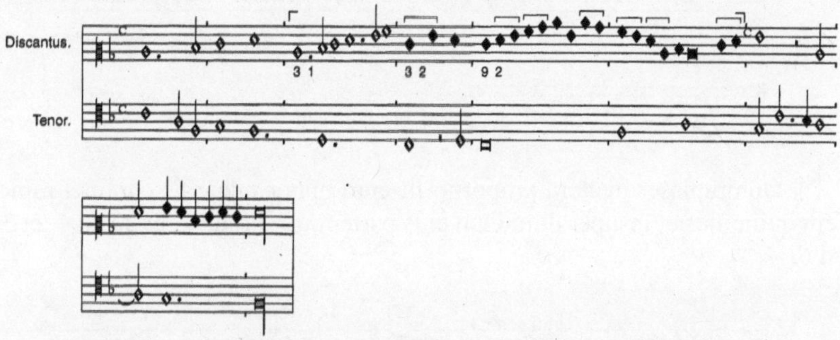

The proportion *quadrupla sesquitertia* occurs when a greater number includes a lesser number four times, as well as a third of the lesser number. For example: 13 to 3, 26 to 6, and 39 to 9. In this proportion, moreover, there are thirteen semibreves against three semibreves, as is notated here:

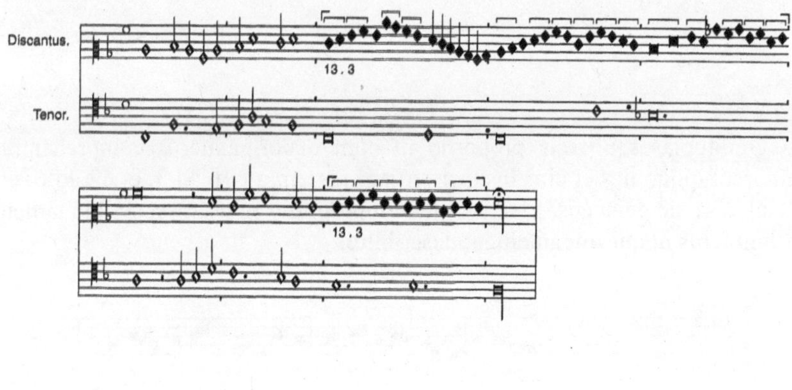

[19]This case of a double inductio (3:1 → 3:2 → 9:2) is unique. It allows the performer to reach *quadrupla sesquialtera* with three much simpler shifts: 3:1, then 1:2, then 3:1 again. See the Introduction, pp. 34–35.

Quadruplasesquiquarta proportio fit cum maior numerus comprehendit minorem quater et insuper eius quartam partem. ut 17 ad 4. et 34 ad 8. et 51 ad 12.

|| Quintuplasesqualtera proportio fit cum maior numerus continet mino- f. 9r
rem quinquies et insuper dimidiam eius partem. ut .11. ad 2. et 22 ad 4. et 33 ad 6.

Quintuplasesquitercia proportio fit cum maior numerus comprehendit minorem quinquies et eius insuper tertiam partem. ut 16 ad 3. et 32 ad 6. et 48 ad 9. et sic deinceps. Etsi hec quidem proportio in usu non sit, hic tamen in cantilenis ut quisque intelligat describitur.

The proportion *quadrupla sesquiquarta* occurs when a greater number includes a lesser number four times, as well as a fourth of the lesser number. For example: 17 to 4, 34 to 8, and 51 to 12.

The proportion *quintupla sesquialtera* occurs when a greater number contains a lesser number five times, as well as half of the lesser number. For example: 11 to 2, 22 to 4, and 33 to 6.

The proportion *quintupla sesquitertia* occurs when a greater number includes a lesser number five times, as well as a third of the lesser number. For example: 16 to 3, 32 to 6, 48 to 9, and so forth in this way. Although this proportion is not used, nevertheless it is notated in the songs here so that everyone can understand it:

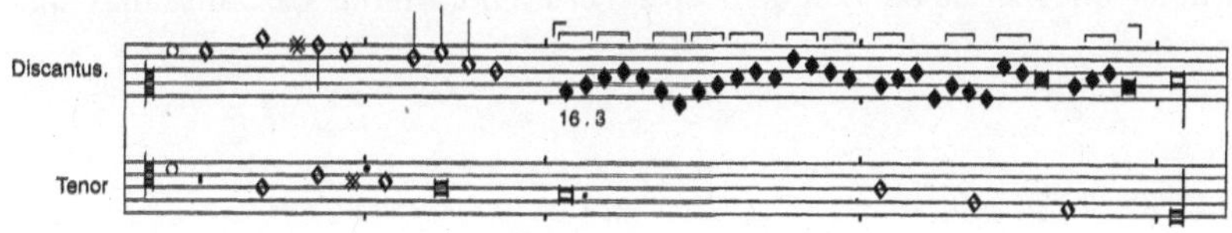

Quintuplasesquiquarta proportio fit cum maior numerus continet minorem quinquies et ⟨eius⟩ insuper quartam partem. ut 21 ad 4. et 42 ad 8. et 63 ad 12. In hac proportione viginti et una semibreves equivalent commensuranturque quatuor semibrevibus ita ut unaqueque ipsarum unius et viginti diminuatur de decemseptem vigessimis primis partibus proprie quantitatis. ut patet hic in notularum ordine.

|| De genere multiplici superparciente et eius speciebus. f. 9v

Multiplexsuperpartiens genus quintum maioris inequalitatis est cum maior numerus ⟨ad minorem⟩ relatus continet ipsum pluries cum una eius aliquanta parte plures aliquotas conducente. Infiniti enim sunt huius generis gradus singulis multiplicibus quascunque superparcientes complectentibus procedentes.

Primus enim gradus fit ex prima multiplici singulis superpartientibus connexa ut duplasuperbipartiens. Duplasupertripartiens. Duplasuperquatripartiens. et deinceps. He enim subalterne species dicuntur. namque in vim generis unaqueque convertitur cum duplarum superbipartientium. Alia duplasuperbipartienstertias. ut 8 ad 3. Alia duplasuperbipartiensquintas. ut 12 ad 5. Alia duplasuperbipartiensseptimas. ut 16 ad 7. Alia duplasuperbipartiensnonas. ut 20 ad 9. et deinceps. Verum huiusmodi specialissimas spe-

2 *scripsi* || 5 de decemseptem vigessimis primis G de consepte primis C || 12 *scripsi* || 16 1us gradus. *in marg.* C ||

The proportion *quintupla sesquiquarta* occurs when a greater number contains a lesser number five times, as well as a fourth of the lesser number. For example: 21 to 4, 42 to 8, and 63 to 12. In this proportion twenty-one semibreves equal and are made commensurate with four semibreves, in such a way that each of the twenty-one is diminished by $^{17}/_{21}$, as is shown in the arrangement of notes here:

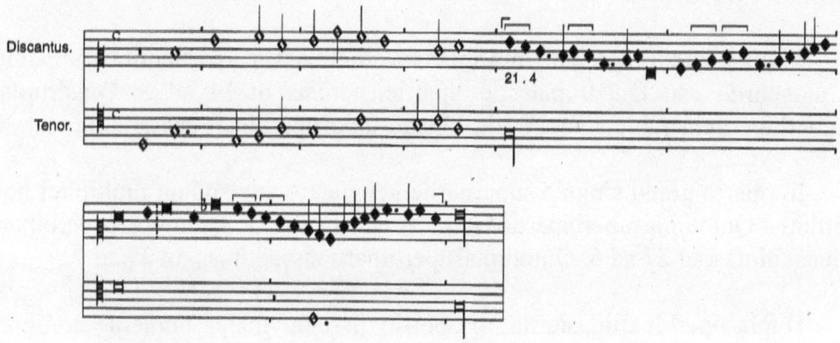

Concerning the *genus multiplex superpartiens* and its species

The *genus multiplex superpartiens*, the fifth *genus* of greater inequality, is when a greater number, in relation to a lesser number, contains the lesser multiple times, along with one of its aliquant parts (which combines several aliquot parts). The degrees of this *genus* are infinite, proceeding from the individual *multiplex* species, each of these covering all *superpartiens* species.

The first degree is made of the first *multiplex* species attached to the individual *superpartiens* species. For example: *dupla superbipartiens*, *dupla supertripartiens*, *dupla superquatripartiens*, and so forth. These are called "alternative species," for each one is adapted to have the effect of a *genus*.[20] In the alternative species *dupla superbipartiens*, one instance is *dupla superbipartiens tertias*, for example 8 to 3; another is *dupla superbipartiens quintas*, for example 12 to 5; another is *dupla superbipartiens septimas*, for example 16 to 7; another is *dupla superbipartiens nonas*, for example 20 to

[20]This introduction of further terminology is meant to accommodate an extra level of divisions: the *genus superpartiens* by itself is already divided into degrees and species and when combined with the *genus multiplex* requires one more classification.

cies vocant. Ceteris vero gradibus consimilis considerationis adhibetur modus.

Secundus gradus singulas superpartientes secunde multiplici coniungit. cuius subalternus et specialissimus ordo est. Triplasuperbipartienstercias. ut .11. ad 3. Triplasuperbipartiensquintas. ut 17 ad 5. Triplasuperbiparciensseptimas. ut 23 ad 7.

Tertius gradus terciam multiplicem singulis superpartientibus apponit. Cuius ordo est. Quadruplasuperbipartienstercias ut 14 ad 3. Quadruplasuperbipartiensquintas. ut 22 ad 5. Quadruplasuperbipartiensseptimas. ut 30 ad 7.

In quarto gradu singule superpartientes quarte applaudunt multiplici hoc ordine. Quintuplasuperbipartienstercias. ut 17 ad 3. Quintuplasuperbipartiensquintas. ut 27 ad 5. Quintuplasuperbipartiensseptimas. ut 37 ad 7.

Duplasuperbipartienstertias proportio fit cum maior numerus comprehendit minorem bis et insuper unam eius aliquantam partem factam ex duabus terciis partibus ipsius minoris. ut 8 ad 3. et 16 ad 6 et 24 ad 9. et deinceps. In hac autem proportione octo semibreves equivalent et commensurantur tribus semibrevibus. ita ut unaqueque ipsarum semibrevium octo diminuatur de quinque octavis partibus proprie quantitatis. et hoc modo componitur. ut hic patet.

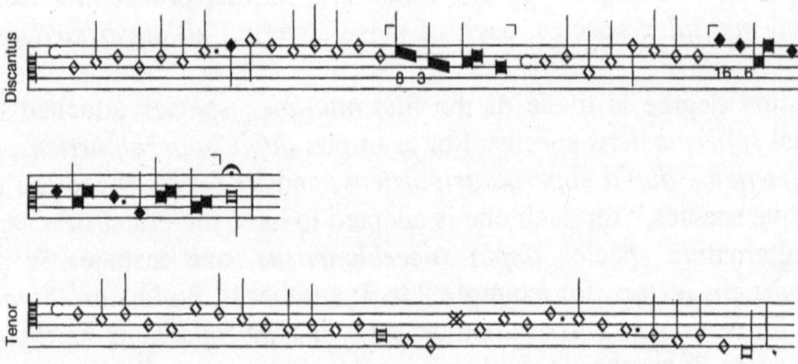

3 2us. *in marg.* C || 7 3us. *in marg.* C | multiplicem]multipli C | superpartientibus]superbipartientibus C || 11 superpartientes]superbipartientes C ||

9; and so forth. But they call instances of this kind "most particular species";[21] a similar manner of consideration, however, is applied to the other degrees.

The second degree conjoins the individual *superpartiens* degrees to the second *multiplex* species. Its alternative and most particular arrangement is: *tripla superbipartiens tertias*, for example 11 to 3; *tripla superbipartiens quintas*, for example 17 to 5; *tripla superbipartiens septimas*, for example 23 to 7.

The third degree adds the third *multiplex* species to the individual *superpartiens* species. Its arrangement is: *quadrupla superbipartiens tertias*, for example 14 to 3; *quadrupla superbipartiens quintas*, for example 22 to 5; *quadrupla superbipartiens septimas*, for example 30 to 7.

In the fourth degree the individual *superpartiens* species complement the fourth *multiplex* species, in this arrangment: *quintupla superbipartiens tertias*, for example 17 to 3; *quintupla superbipartiens quintas*, for example 27 to 5; *quintupla superbipartiens septimas*, for example 37 to 7.

The proportion *dupla superbipartiens tertias* occurs when a greater number includes a lesser number twice, as well as an aliquant part made of two thirds of the lesser number. For example: 8 to 3, 16 to 6, 24 to 9, and so forth. In this proportion, moreover, eight semibreves equal and are made commensurate with three semibreves, in such a way that each of the eight semibreves is diminished by five eighths of its own quantity. It is composed in the way shown here:

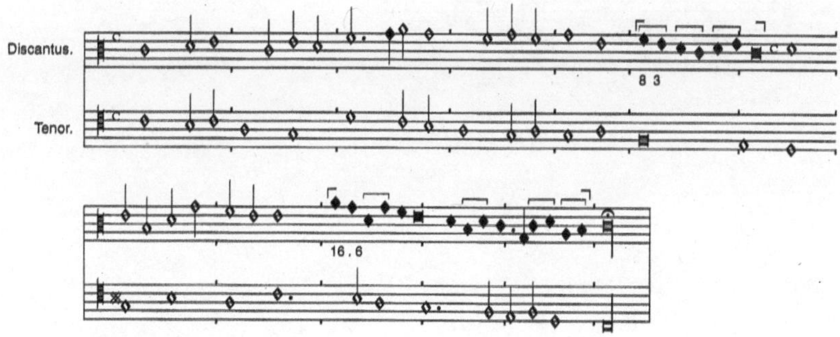

[21]The *specialissima species* ("most particular species") is Gaffurius's final level of classification for the *genus multiplex superpartiens.* The overall division of this *genus*, therefore, is as follows: (1) degree, e.g., *dupla superpartiens*; (2) alternative species, e.g., *dupla superbipartiens*; and (3) most particular species, e.g., *dupla superbipartiens tertias.*

|| Duplasuperbipartiensquintas proportio fit cum maior numerus continet minorem bis et insuper duas eius quintas partes. ut 12 ad 5. et 24 ad 10. et 36 ad 15. Hec autem proportio duodecim semibreves equifacit quinque semibrevibus. ut hic in cantilenis figuratur. f. 10r

Duplasupertripartiensquartas proportio fit cum maior numerus comprehendit minorem bis et insuper tres eius quartas partes. ut 11 ad 4. et 22 ad 8. et 33 ad 12.

---

3 equifacit]equi facit C || 5 m. 4: O]C C | m. 6: O]C C ||

The proportion *dupla superbipartiens quintas* occurs when a greater number contains a lesser number twice, as well as two fifths of the lesser number. For example: 12 to 5, 24 to 10, and 36 to 15. This proportion, moreover, makes twelve semibreves equal to five semibreves, as is written out in the cantilena here:

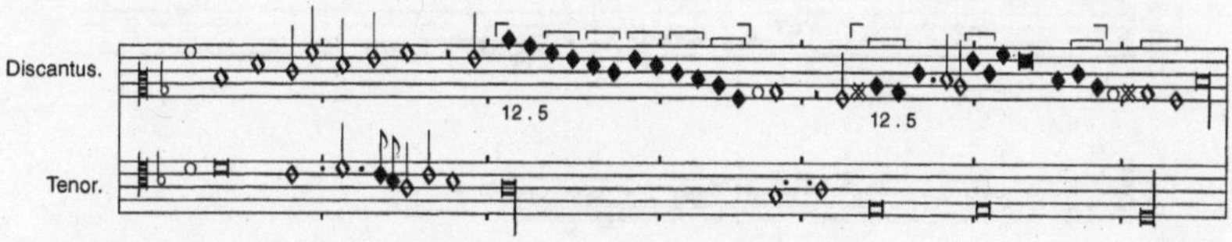

The proportion *dupla supertripartiens quartas* occurs when a greater number contains a lesser number twice, as well as three fourths of the lesser number. For example: 11 to 4, 22 to 8, and 33 to 12.

Duplasupertriparciensquintas proportio fit cum maior numerus continet minorem bis et tres eius quintas partes. ut 13 ad 5. et 26 ad 10 et 39 ad 15. Hec autem proportio tresdecim semibreves in temporis mensura quinque semibrevibus coequat ut hic describitur.

|| Triplasuperbipartienstertias proportio fit cum maior numerus continet minorem ter et insuper duas eius tercias partes. ut 11 ad 3. et 22 ad 6. et 33 ad 9. In hac proportione undecim semibreves equivalent et commensurantur tribus semibrevibus. ut hic in notularum ordine. f. 10v

The proportion *dupla supertripartiens quintas* occurs when a greater number contains a lesser number twice, and three fifths of the lesser number. For example: 13 to 5, 26 to 10, and 39 to 15. This proportion, moreover, regards thirteen semibreves as equivalent to five semibreves in measure of time, as is notated here:

The proportion *tripla superbipartiens tertias* occurs when a greater number contains a lesser number three times, as well as two thirds of the lesser number. For example: 11 to 3, 22 to 6, and 33 to 9. In this proportion, eleven semibreves equal and are made commensurate with three semibreves, as in the arrangement of notes here:

Triplasuperbipartiensquintas proportio fit cum maior numerus continet minorem ter et insuper duas ipsius quintas partes. ut 17 ad 5. et 34 ad 10. In hac proportione decem et septem semibreves quinque semibrevibus equivalent et commensurantur. ut hic describitur.

|| Triplasupertripartiensquartas proportio fit cum maior numerus continet minorem ter et tres eius quartas partes. ut 15 ad 4. et 30 ad 8. et 45 ad 12. f. 11r
Hec autem proportio quindecim semibreves quatuor semibrevibus equat. ut hic in notulis figuratur.

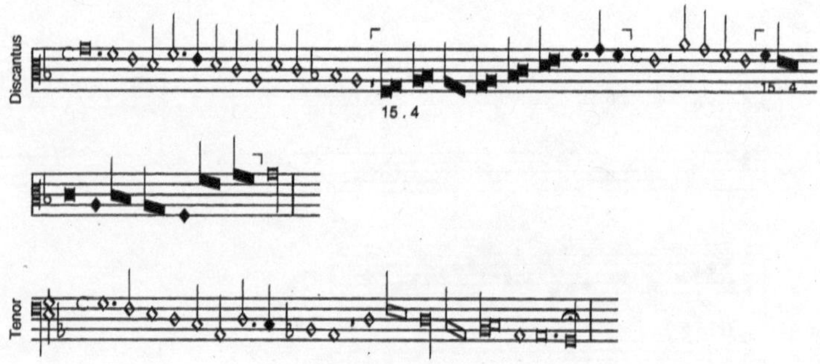

8 Triplasupertripartiensquartas] TTriplasupertripartiensquartas C ||

The proportion *tripla superbipartiens quintas* occurs when a greater number contains a lesser number three times, as well as two fifths of the lesser number. For example, 17 to 5 and 34 to 10. In this proportion, seventeen semibreves equal and are made commensurate with five semibreves, as is notated here:

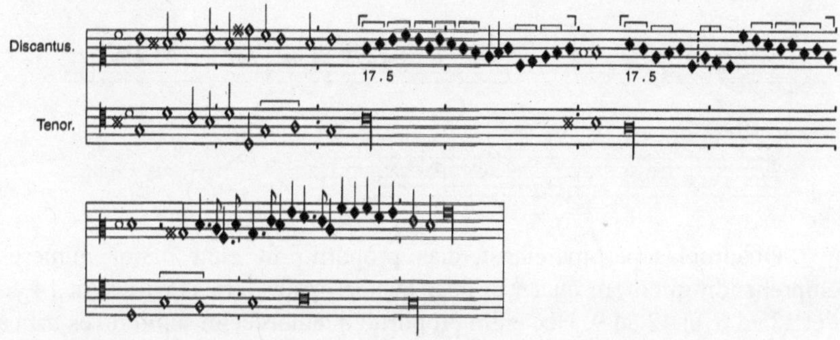

The proportion *tripla supertripartiens quartas* occurs when a greater number contains a lesser number three times, and three fourths of the lesser. For example: 15 to 4, 30 to 8, and 45 to 12. This proportion, moreover, equates fifteen semibreves with four semibreves, as is written out in the notes here:

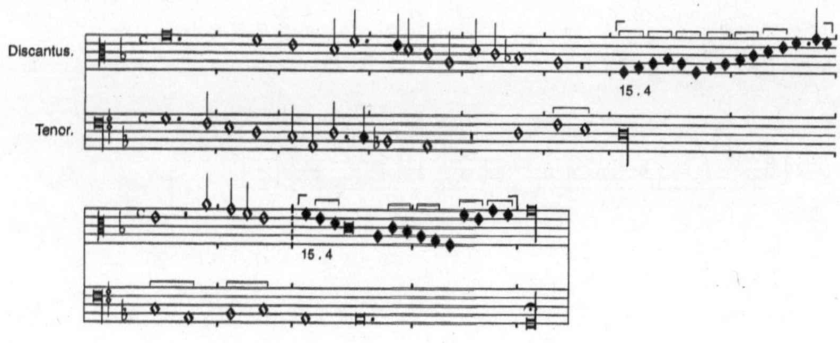

Triplasupertripartiensquintas proporcio fit cum maior numerus comprehendit minorem ter et insuper tres eius quintas partes. ut 18 ad 5. et 36 ad 10. et 54 ad 15. Hec autem proportio decem et octo semibreves quinque semibrevibus equefacit ita ut unaqueque ipsarum decem et octo diminuatur de tresdecim octodenis partibus proprie quantitatis. et hoc modo describitur.

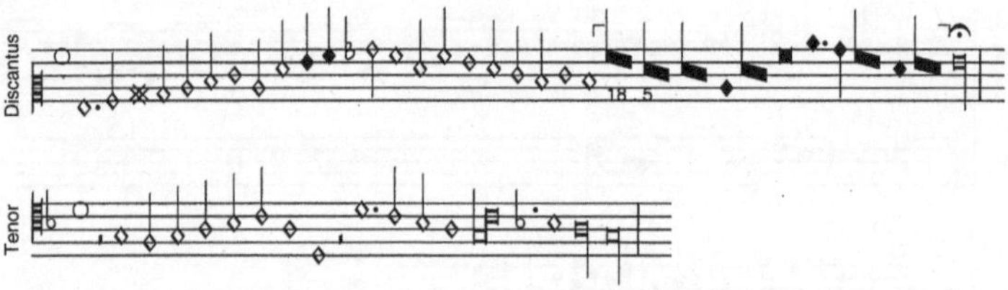

|| Quadruplasuperbiparcienstercias proportio fit cum maior numerus comprehendit minorem quater et duas insuper ipsius tercias partes. ut 14 ad 3. et 28 ad 6. et 42 ad 9. Hec enim proportio quatuordecim semibreves tribus semibrevibus coequat in potencia temporis et mensura. ita ut singulaqueque ipsarum quatuordecim diminuatur de undecim quartisdecimis partibus sui valoris. ut hic notatur. f. 11v

1 Triplasupertripartiensquintas]TTriplasupertripartiensquintas C || 11 in potencia]inpotencia C || 13 valoris]maioris C ||

The proportion *tripla supertripartiens quintas* occurs when a greater number includes a lesser number three times, as well as three fifths of the lesser number. For example, 18 to 5, 36 to 10, and 54 to 15. This proportion, moreover, makes eighteen semibreves equal to five semibreves, in such a way that each of the eighteen is diminished by thirteen eighteenths of its own quantity. It is notated in this way:

The proportion *quadrupla superbipartiens tertias* occurs when a greater number includes a lesser number four times, as well as two thirds of the lesser number. For example: 14 to 3, 28 to 6, and 42 to 9. This proportion regards fourteen semibreves as equivalent to three semibreves in effect and measure of time, in such a way that every one of the fourteen is diminished by eleven fourteenths of its value, as is recorded here:

Quadruplasuperbipartiensquintas proportio fit cum maior numerus comprehendit minorem quater cum duabus eius quintis partibus ut. 22 ad 5. et 44 ad 10. et 66 ad 15. Hec autem proportio viginti et duas semibreves quinque semibrevibus coequat. ut in cantilenis hic notatur.

2 quater]quatuor C ||

The proportion *quadrupla superbipartiens quintas* occurs when a greater number includes a lesser number four times, along with two fifths of the lesser number. For example: 22 to 5, 44 to 10, and 66 to 15. This proportion, moreover, regards twenty-two semibreves as equivalent to five semibreves, as is recorded in the cantilena here:

|| Quadruplasupertripartiensquartas proportio fit cum maior numerus comprehendit minorem quater et insuper tres ipsius quartas partes. ut 19 ad 4. et 38 ad 8. et 57 ad 12. Hec autem proportio decem ac novem semibreves quatuor semibrevibus connumerat et commensurat. ita ut unaquaeque ipsarum decemnovem diminuatur de quindecim decimis⟨nonis⟩ partibus proprie quantitatis. ut hoc percipitur concentu. f. 12r

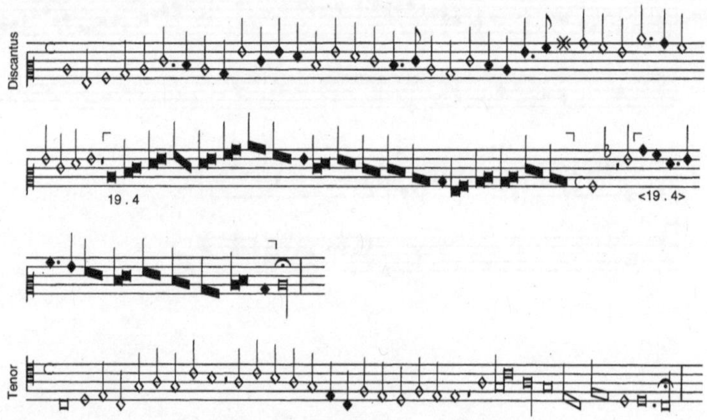

Quod Joannes Dygonus Modo Vuylborus.

5 *scripsi* || 8 *scripsi* ||

The proportion *quadrupla supertripartiens quartas* occurs when a greater number includes a lesser number four times, as well as three fourths of the lesser number. For example: 19 to 4, 38 to 8, and 57 to 12. This proportion, moreover, counts and makes commensurate nineteen semibreves with four semibreves, in such a way that each of the nineteen is diminished by fifteen nineteenths of its own quantity, as is perceived in this piece:

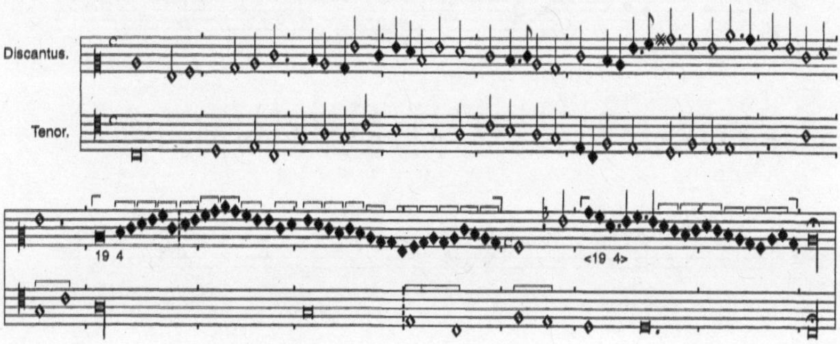

Quod John Dygon, now Wylbore[22]

[22]The term "quod" in this context has no simple translation into English and in fact appears at the close of vernacular texts as well as Latin (e.g., **GB**-Lbl Lansdowne 763, f. 113^{r}). While the modern term "by" would have an authorial implication, "quod" could denote simple scribal activity, as well as authorship or, in the present case, a form of editorial work and revision. The second name, Wylbore, is an alias taken up by Dygon after the dissolution of St. Augustine's monastery in July 1538. See the Introduction, pp. 16–19.

|| ⟨INCIPIT TRACTATUS SECUNDUS⟩ f. 13r

Proportio dupla est prima species multiplicis generis. in qua maior notularum numerus aequivalet minori. ut hisce semicirculis in presentis concentus descriptione notatur.

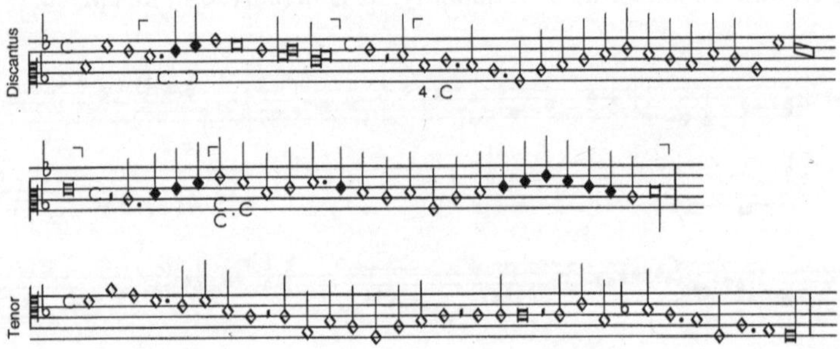

---

1 *scripsi* ||

HERE BEGINS THE SECOND TREATISE

The proportion *dupla* is the first species of the *genus multiplex*. In this proportion a greater number of notes equals a lesser number,[23] as is recorded with these semicircles in the notation of the present piece:[24]

[23]This definition of *dupla* represents a partial copy of the definition given in the first treatise (pp. 68–71 *supra*), which is rendered extremely vague through the lack of the next phrase: "in such a way that every note of the greater number is diminished by half of its quantity." The remainder of the treatise does away with any attempt to define the proportions (or genera); this groundwork has already been laid out in the first treatise.

[24]The use of mensuration signs ("semicircles") as markers for proportions in place of Hindu-Arabic numerals follows a highly unusual format in this treatise, in which signs are translated into numeric values and then added and compared. The only traces of a similar usage are encountered in John Tucke's notebook (**GB**-Lbl Add. 10336). Dygon nowhere explains how his system is derived, but the pattern is regular and discernable; for an explanation of the mechanics of the system and its relation to Tucke's text, see the Introduction, pp. 48–57. The juxtaposition of the numeral 4 and the symbol C in this example (as in several others) confirms the numerical interpretation of the mensuration signs in the treatise.

|| Tripla proportio est secunda species multiplicis generis. que variis f. 13v
modis vel per semibrevem vel per minimam hic in cantilenis describitur.

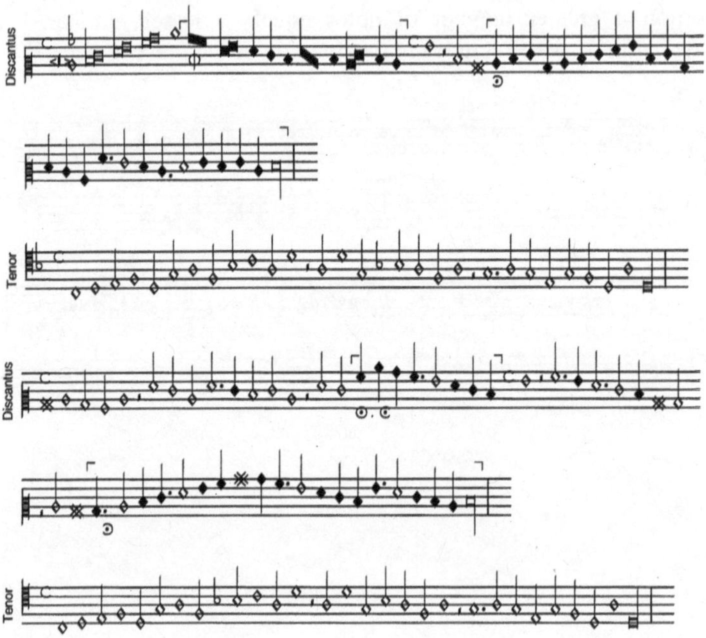

3 *scripsi* || 6–8 Tripla per minimam. *in marg.* C ||

The proportion *tripla* is the second species of the *genus multiplex*. This proportion is notated in various manners in the cantilena here, either at the level of the semibrevis or at the level of the minima:[25]

[25]The first two signs used for proportions in this example, ⦶ and Ͽ, fall outside the regular system demonstrated in the treatise. Like the sign Ↄ for sesquitertia (see pp. 144–45 *infra*), they were used in actual practice and are signalled for this reason by Dygon (see the Introduction, pp. 51–52). The sign ⦶, of course, does not indicate *tripla* in and of itself, but in the present example, the combination of diminution by half, *tempus perfectum*, and brevis equivalence produces the same result: three semibreves in the Discantus against one in the Tenor.

The comparison of the signs ⊙ and Ͼ as 9 to 3 in the second example is also something of an inconsistency, since ⊙ as nine minimae represents the number of minimae in a brevis under ⊙, whereas 3 represents the number of minimae in a semibrevis under Ͼ. The latter is Dygon's usual method of calculation, but anytime the symbol ⊙ is used in the treatise, it represents nine minimae. For the present case, Dygon needed to represent 9:3 minimae rather than 3:1, since he had devised no symbol that could represent one minima, in the way that Ↄ represents one semibrevis. It is unclear why the theorist chose not to use Ͽ for this purpose; although the symbol is used by itself as a sign of *tripla*, likewise Ↄ by itself signifies *sesquitertia.*

Note continues on p. 141

|| Quadrupla proportio quam hisce semicirculis et per semibrevem et per minimam componere solemus ut hic. f. 14r

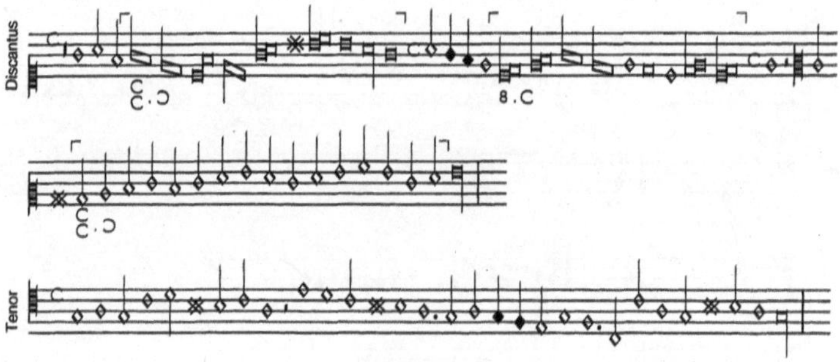

Quintupla semper per semibrevem. ut hic.

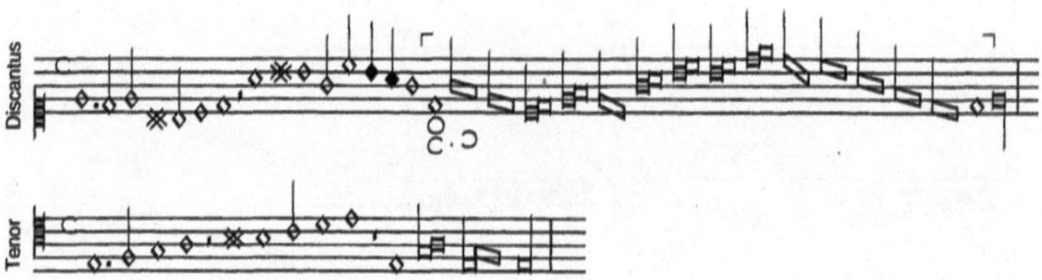

This is the proportion *quadrupla*, which we are accustomed to compose with these semicircles both at the level of the semibrevis and at the level of the minima, as here:

Quintupla is always at the level of the semibrevis, as here:

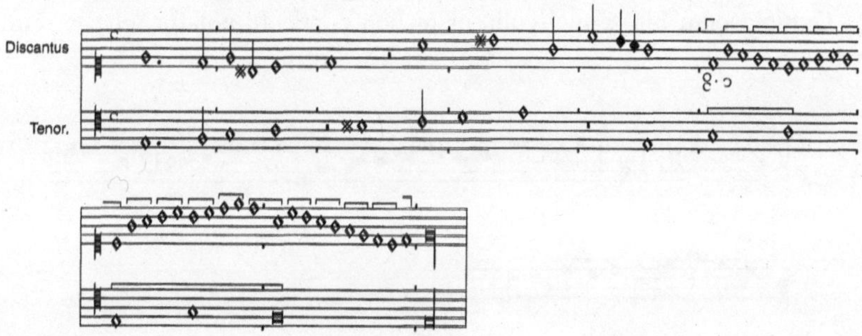

Both examples use the same Tenor. The sequential opening of the Tenor against the rising scale of the Discanus in the first example suggests that the Tenor was originally composed with the first Discantus and reused for the next example.

Sextupla et semper per semibrevem ut in hoc hisce semicirculus concentu notatur.

Septupla raro aut nunquam in usu est. si volueris. accipe ut supra cum f. 14v
figuris. et his quidem modis frui possis. ut hic CCO ad Ↄ et semper per semibrevem.

Octupla cum his semicirculis ut in hoc concentu notatur. et per semibrevem.

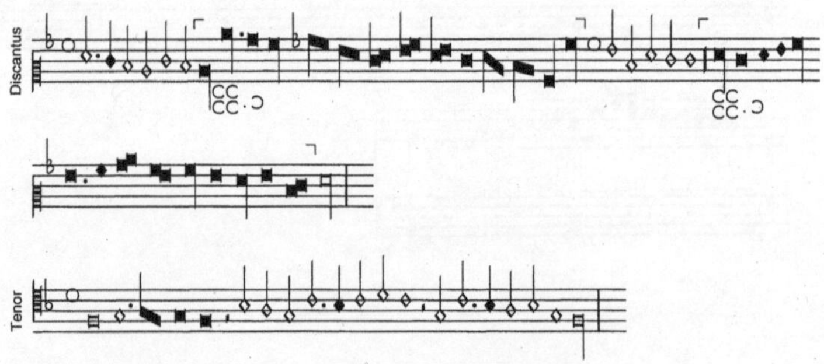

Satis de genere multiplici.

Sextupla is always at the level of the semibrevis, as is recorded with these semicircles in this piece:

Septupla is rarely or never used. If you would like to use it, undertake it with symbols as above. You should be able to use these methods, as here: CCO against Ɔ, and always at the level of the semibrevis.[26]

Octupla is recorded in this piece with these semicircles, at the level of the semibrevis:

Enough concerning the *genus multiplex.*

---

[26]This is the only case in the manuscript of a proportion being explained without a musical example, although Dygon states that other proportions he demonstrates are not in use (pp. 146–47 *infra*). An example of *septupla* appears in the first treatise (pp. 78–79 *supra*).

De genere superparticulari.

Sesqualtera per semibrevem ut 3. semibreves ad duas hoc pacto O ad C et per minimam ut novem minime ad sex minimas ut hic per hos circulos ⊙ ad O et 3. minime ad duas minimas per hos semicirculos Ͼ ad C.

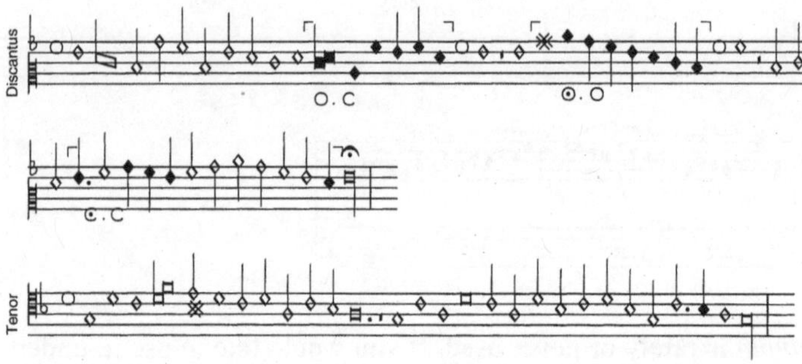

|| Sesquitertia ut quatuor minime ad tres minimas et hoc quidem semicirculo semper utimur ut hic Ɔ et notule, uti presens probat concentus, nigre sint et plene. f. 15r

Hos quidam fortasse semicirculos pro hac proportione sesquitercia uolunt ut hic CC ad Ͼ set, ut prescripsi, facias velim si recte hanc proportionem sesquitertiam componere volueris.

Concerning the *genus superparticulare*

Sesquialtera is both at the level of the semibrevis, for example: three semibreves against two in this way: O against C; and at the level of the minima, for example: nine minimae against six minimae, as shown through these circles: ⊙ against O; and three minimae against two minimae, through these semicircles: Ͼ against C.[27]

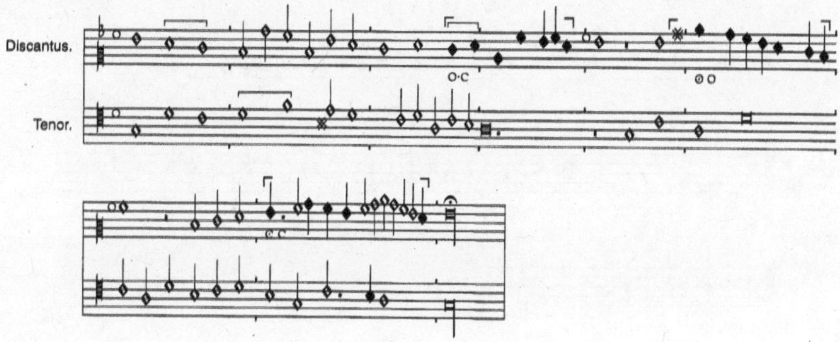

Sesquitertia is, for example: four minimae against three minimae. We always use this semicircle here: Ɔ; and the notes (as the present piece verifies) should be black and "full":[28]

Perhaps, for this proportion *sesquitertia*, some want to use these semicircles here: CC against Ͼ; but you should do as I have written above if you would like to compose this proportion *sesquitertia* correctly.

---

[27]The comparison here of ⊙ against O is the only case in which O is used to represent a value in minimae (like ⊙, derived unusually from the number of minimae in the brevis rather than semibrevis).

[28]The specification of color for this proportion is unique in Dygon's treatises and by no means accidental. This demonstration of *sesquitertia* and the example of the same proportion in the first treatise (pp. 82–83 *supra*) are the only instances of black full notation in the manuscript. The use of Ɔ here falls outside the regular system being described in the treatise (as Dygon notes immediately below the example) but corresponds to standard notational practice known both in England and on the Continent since the late fourteenth century.

Sesquiquarta his modis per semibrevem OC ad CC et per minimam ϾC ad CC frui possis. Verum hec proportio sesquiquarta et que huius generis superparticularis sequuntur in usu non sunt.

|| Sesquiquinta per semibrevem hos quidem circulos habet ut hic OO ad OC et per minimam ut ϾϾ ad ϾC f. 15v

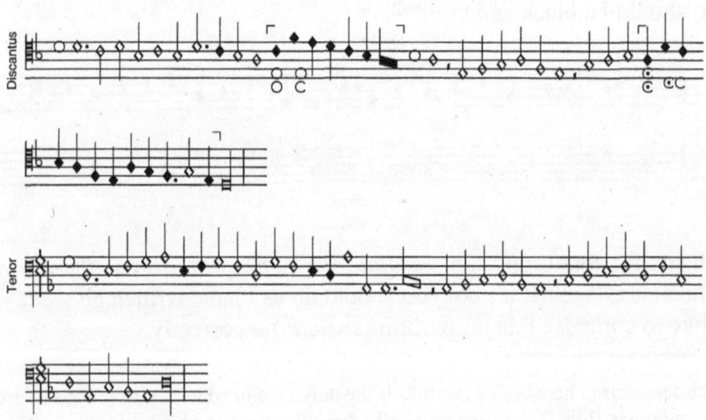

3 sequuntur]sequntur C ||

You should be able to use *sesquiquarta* with these methods: at the level of the semibrevis, OC against CC; and at the level of the minima, ϾC against CC. This proportion *sesquiquarta*, however, and those of this *genus superparticulare* which follow, are not used.

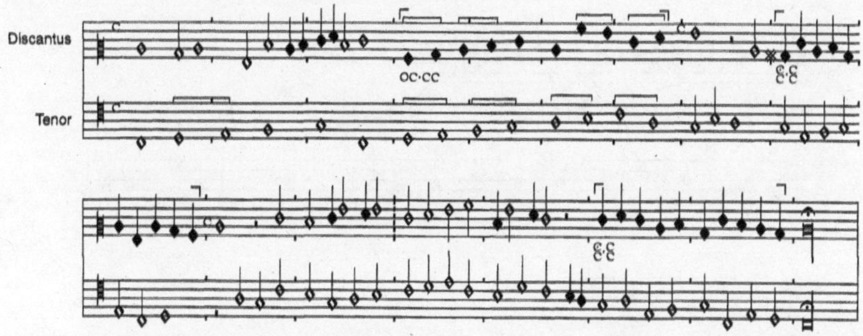

Sesquiquinta at the level of the semibrevis has these circles here: OO against OC; and at the level of the minima: ϾϾ against ϾC.

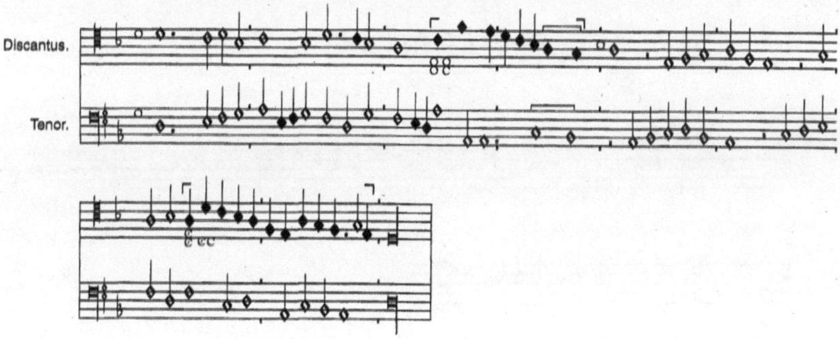

Sesquisexta per minimam.

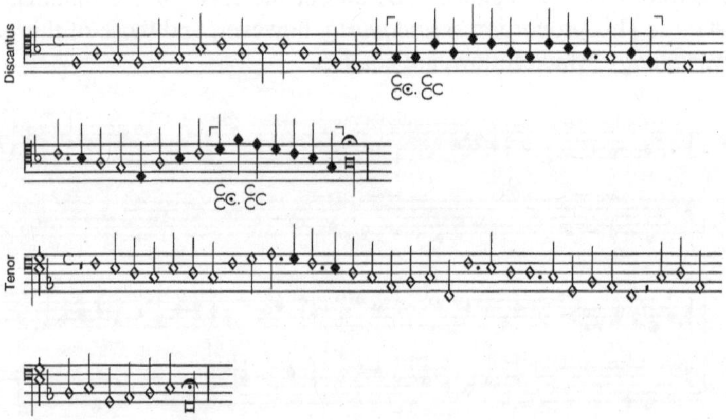

Sesquiseptima per minimam.

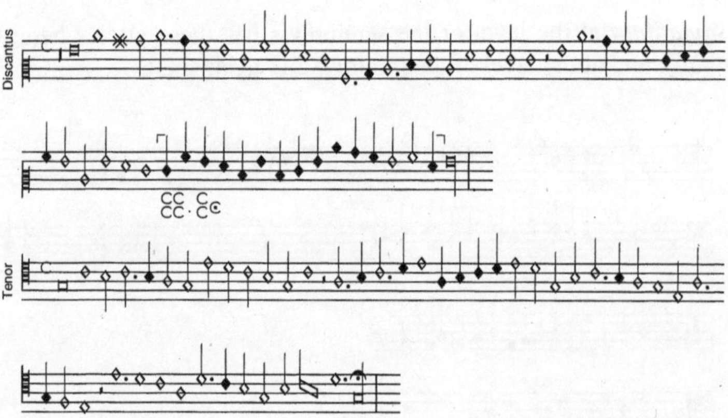

Sesquisexta at the level of the minima:

Sesquiseptima at the level of the minima:

|| Sesquioctava. per minimam. f. 16r

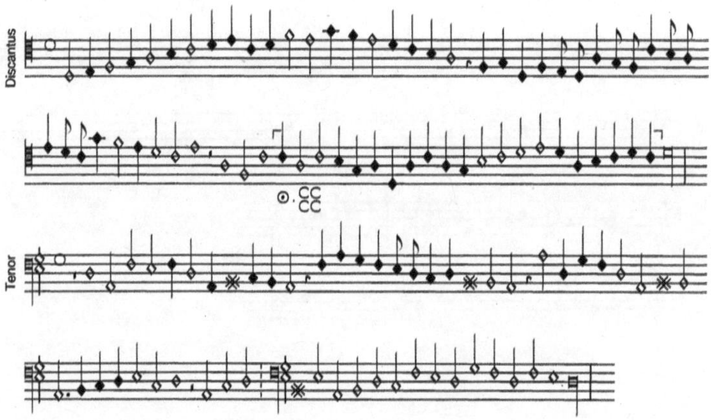

De genere superpartienti.

Superbipartienstertias hos quidem circulos habet per semibrevem. OC ad O et per minimam ut hic ⊙C ad ⊙.

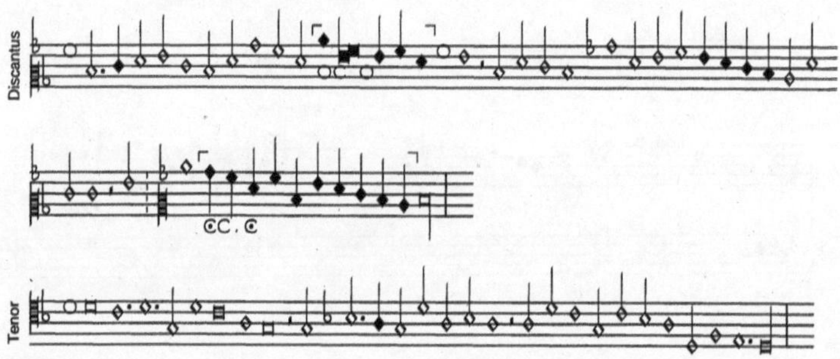

Sesquioctava at the level of the minima:

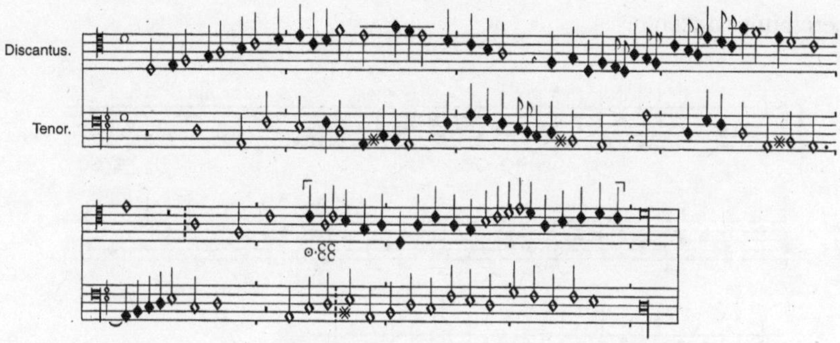

Concerning the *genus superpartiens*

Superbipartiens tertias has these circles at the level of the semibrevis: ○C against ○; and at the level of the minima: ⊙C against ⊙.

|| Superbipartiensquintas sub hac forma per semibrevem ut hic CCO ad OC et per minimam hos accipias velim semicirculos. CCͼ ad ͼC ut hoc percipitur concentu. f. 16v

De genere multiplicisuperparticulari et eius speciebus.

Duplasesqualtera est prima species huius generis multiplicissuperparticularis et his characteribus utitur ut hic. OC ad C. hoc est quinque semibreves ad duas. vel per minimam ut hic. ͼC ad C. hoc est 5 𝅗𝅥 ad 2 minimas.

Superbipartiens quintas appears in this form at the level of the semibrevis: CCO against OC; and at the level of the minima, you should make use of these semicircles: CCϾ against ϾC, as is perceived in this piece:

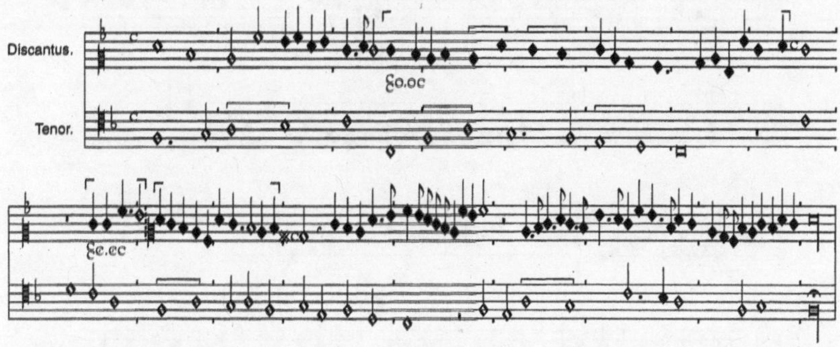

Concerning the *genus multiplex superparticulare* and its species

Dupla sesquialtera is the first species of this *genus multiplex superparticulare*, and it uses these characters: OC against C, that is, five semibreves against two; or at the level of the minima, as here: ϾC against C, that is, five ♩ against two minimae.

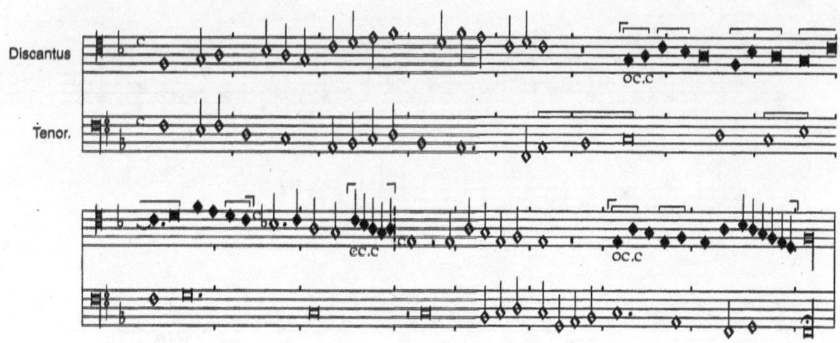

|| Duplasesquitercia per minimam ut hic CC𝇊 ad 𝇊 et per semibrevem ut hic CCO ad O ut in ordine nọtularum hic patet. f. 17r

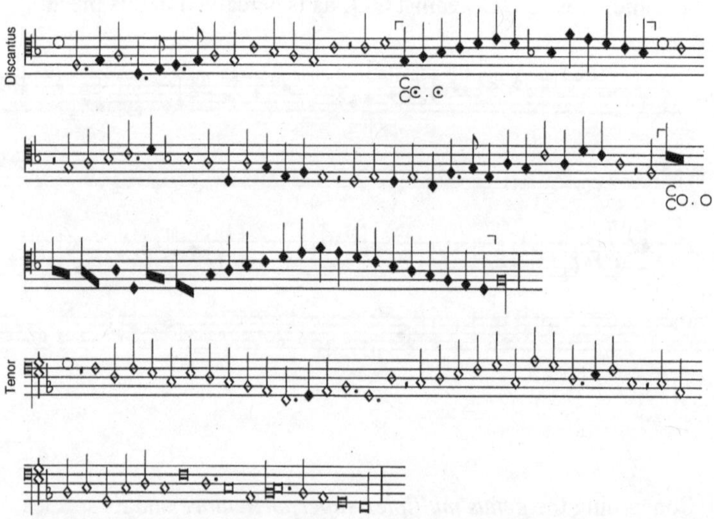

Duplasesquiquarta per minimam ut patet hic. ⊙ ad CC.

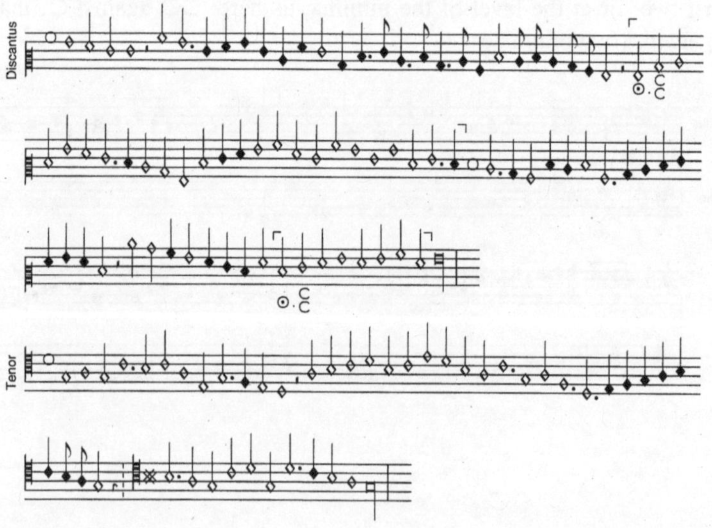

3 m. 5: O]C C ||

Dupla sesquitertia at the level of the minima is as here: CCĊ against Ċ; and at the level of the semibrevis as here: CCO against O, as is shown in the arrangement of notes here:

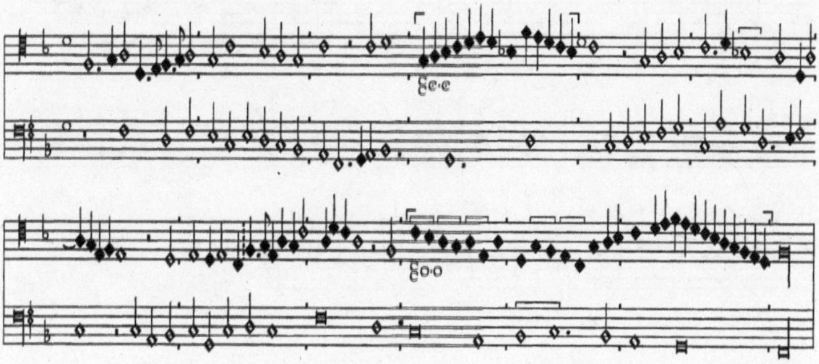

Dupla sesquiquarta at the level of the minima is as shown here: ⊙ against CC.

|| Triplasesqualtera per semibrevem ut hic CCO ad C et per minimam f. 17v
per hos semicirculos CCϾ ad C.

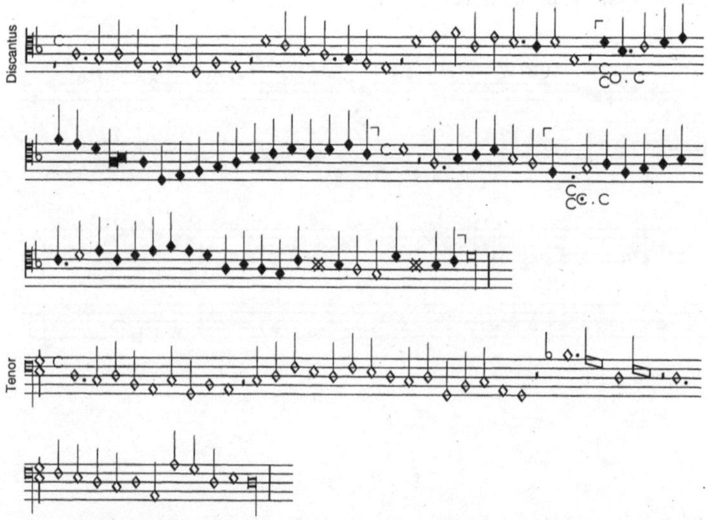

Quadruplasesqualtera hoc quidem circulo per semibrevem utimur ut hic O in quo modus perfectus 9 semibreves sibi vendicat. et per minimam ut hic ⊙ C ut in cantilenis notatur.

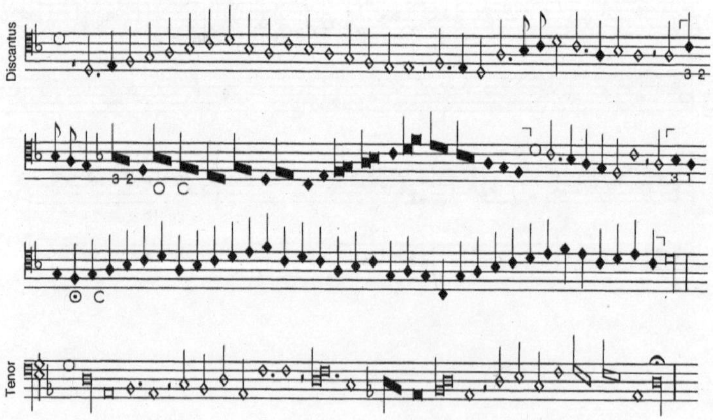

Tripla sesquialtera at the level of the semibrevis is as shown here: CCO against C; and at the level of the minima through these semicircles: CCĊ against C.

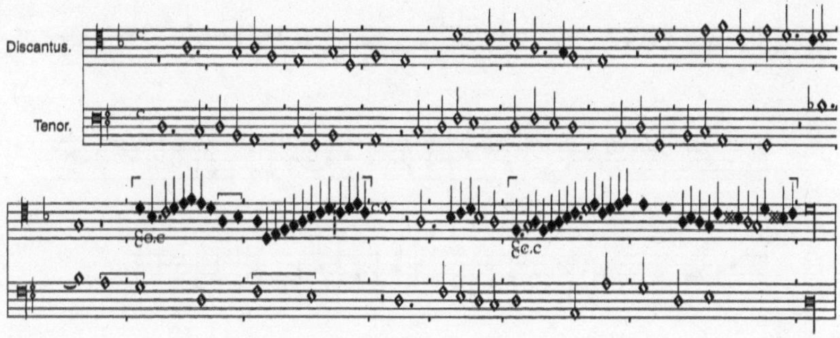

We use *quadrupla sesquialtera* at the level of the semibrevis with this circle here: O. In this proportion *modus perfectus* claims nine semibreves for itself.[29] At the level of the minima, it is as here: ⊙ C, as is recorded in these cantilena:

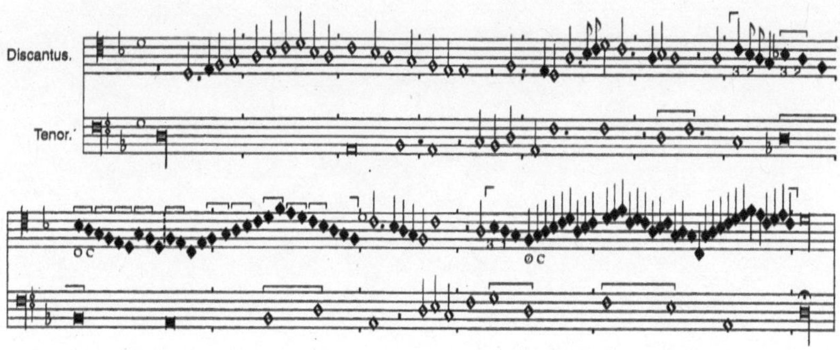

---

[29]Dygon attempts here to use the single mensuration sign O as an indicator of "perfect minor mood" but falls into inconsistency, as the combination O C was already used to indicate 3:2 at the level of the semibrevis (pp. 144–45 *supra*). In treating *modus minor* as perfect under O (i.e., the longa is divided into three breves), Dygon sides with Gaffurius and other continental writers against the opposite British practice, as described by the Scot-

|| Duplasuperbipartienstercias per semibrevem ut hic CCCC ad O aut f. 18r
hoc pacto per minimam ut hic CCCC ad Ͼ aut per figuram ut hic. 8 ad O. 8 ad Ͼ.

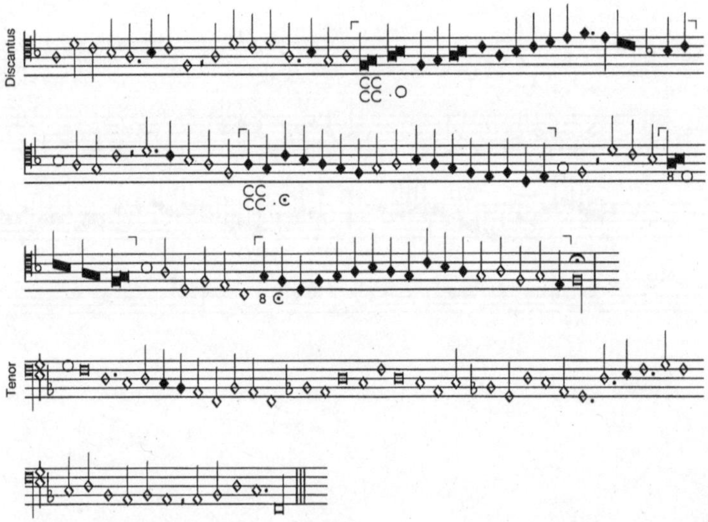

Dupla superbipartiens tertias at the level of the semibrevis is as here: CCCC against O; or at the level of the minima in this way: CCCC against Ͼ, or through a symbol as here: 8 against O; 8 against Ͼ.

tish Anonymous: "Heir is ane gryth varience betuix the Bretans and utheris musicians of dyverss regionis annentis the muid perfyt of the less in this wyiss. The docturis of music, sic as Gaforus Laudensis, Faber Strabulen, Wolicus Baroducensis with dyverss uther doctouris dois writt that in the long of the muid less perfyt thrie brevis ar contenit, and the paus of the long dois occupie four levillis and in haill spacis in the maner following .... Quhilk Britans maner, to all doctouris contrary, for quhy thay consider bot tua brevis contenit in the long of the muid perfyt of the less and the pauss of the long dois occupie bot thrie levilis and tua spacis in this maner ..." (**GB**-Lbl Add. 4911, ff. 5^{v}–6^{r}; edited in Judson Maynard, "An Anonymous Scottish Treatise on Music from the Sixteenth Century, British Museum Additional Manuscript 4911, Edition and Commentary," 2 vols. [Ph.D. dissertation, Indiana University, 1961], 2:13–14).

APPENDIX

John Dygon, Surviving Motet Extracts (**GB**-Lbl R.M. 24.d.2, ff. 165v–166r)

1. *Ad lapidis posicionem / quod enim vivit*

8
re non servabant pe -
re non servabant pe - nam iusti -
servabant pe - nam,
12
nam iusti - ci -
ci -
iusti - ci -
15

18
e:.
e:.
e.
21
quod
e -
quod e -
quod
26
nim, vi -
nim vi -
e nim, vi - vit, vi -

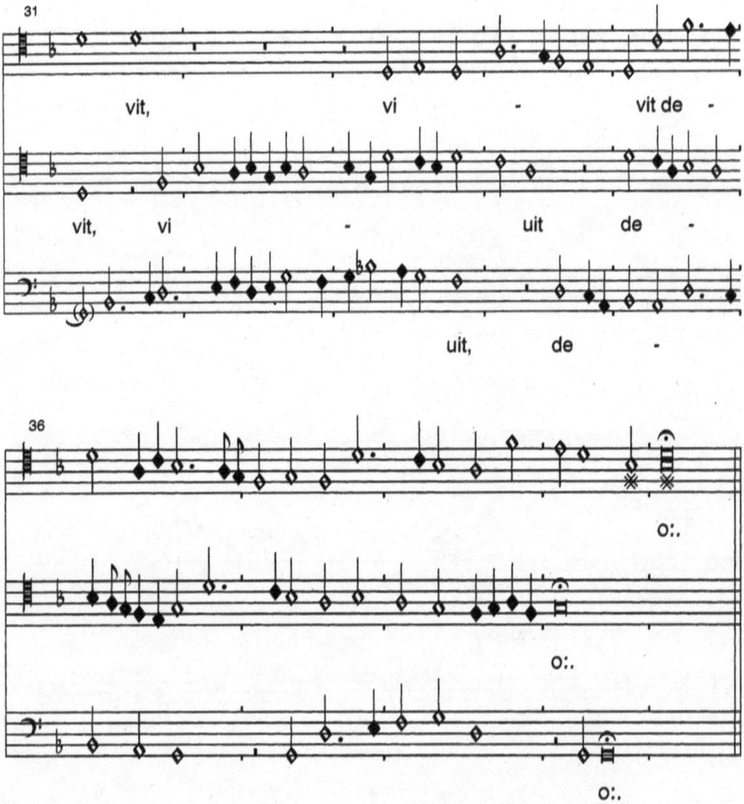
31
vit, vi - vit de -
vit, vi - uit de -
uit, de -
36
o:.
o:.
o:.

2. *Rex benedicte / vt tergant miseras / atque colant*

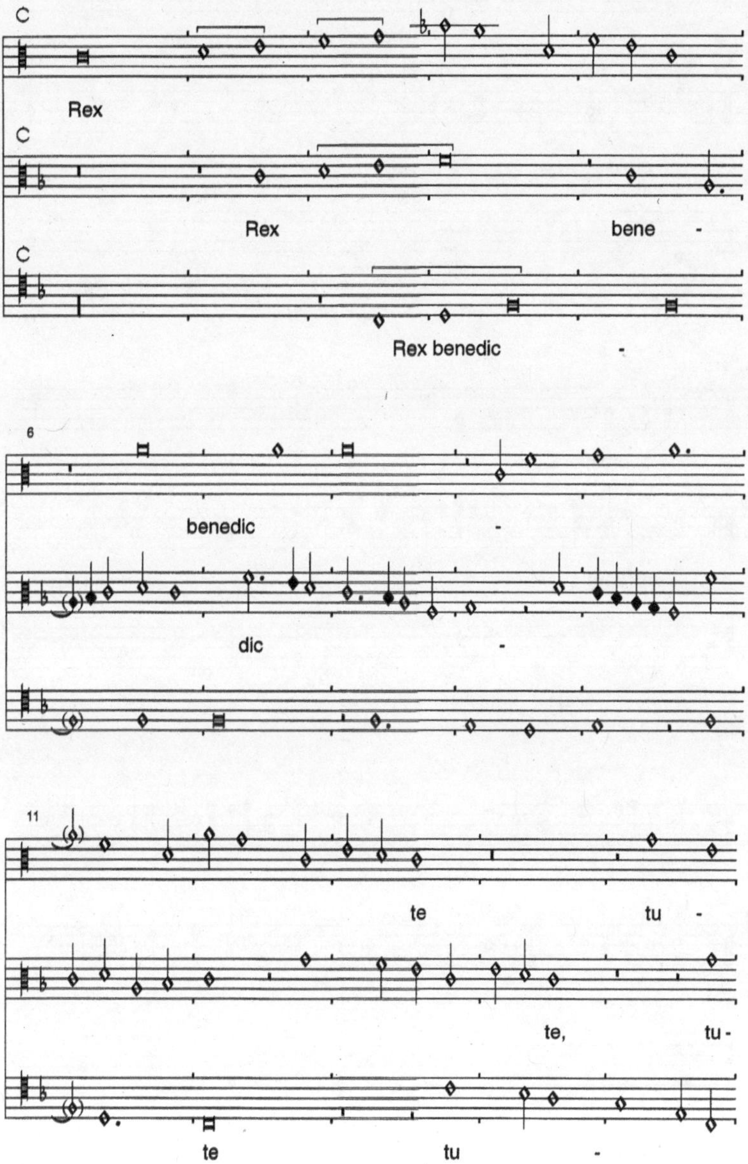

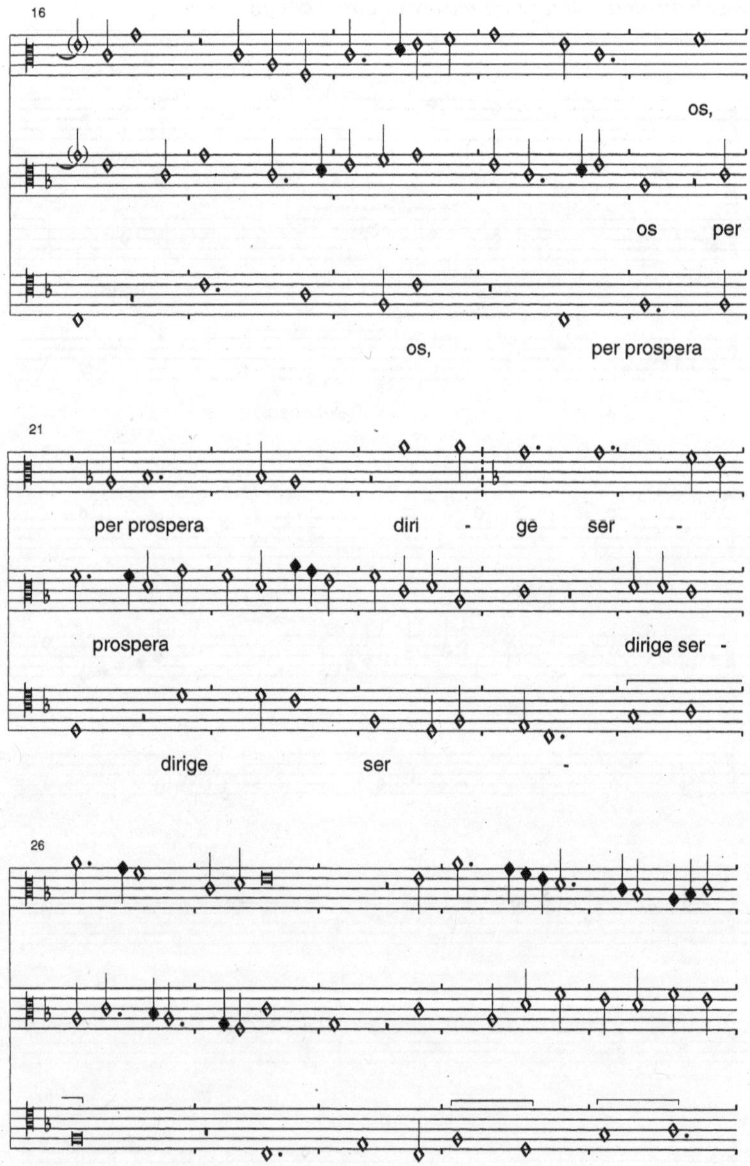
16
os,
os per
os, per prospera
21
per prospera diri - ge ser -
prospera dirige ser -
dirige ser -
26

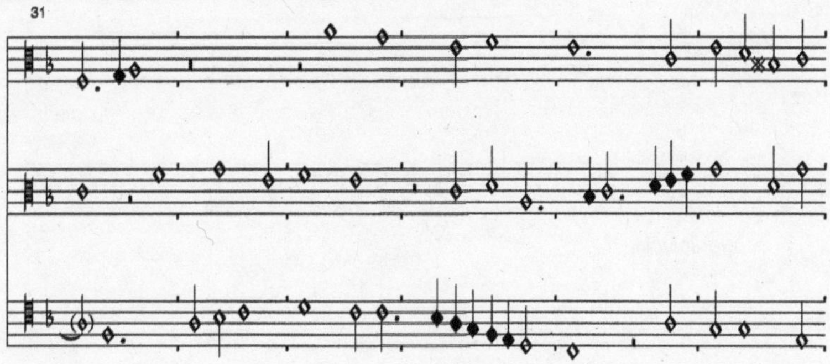

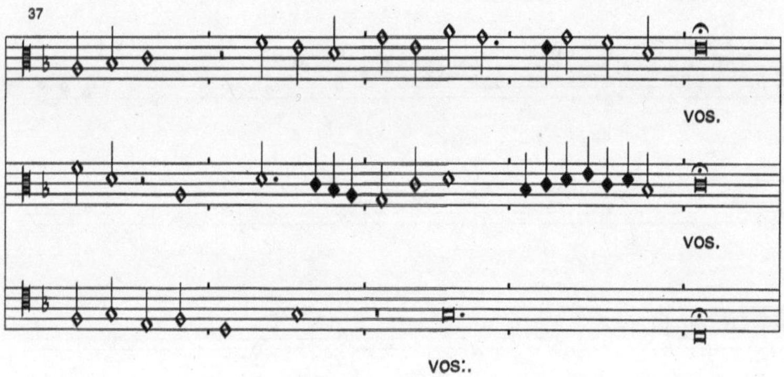
vos.
vos.
vos:.

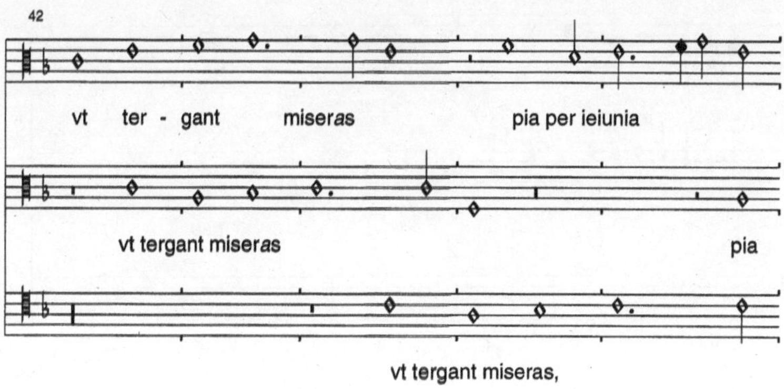
vt ter - gant miseras pia per ieiunia
vt tergant miseras pia
vt tergant miseras,

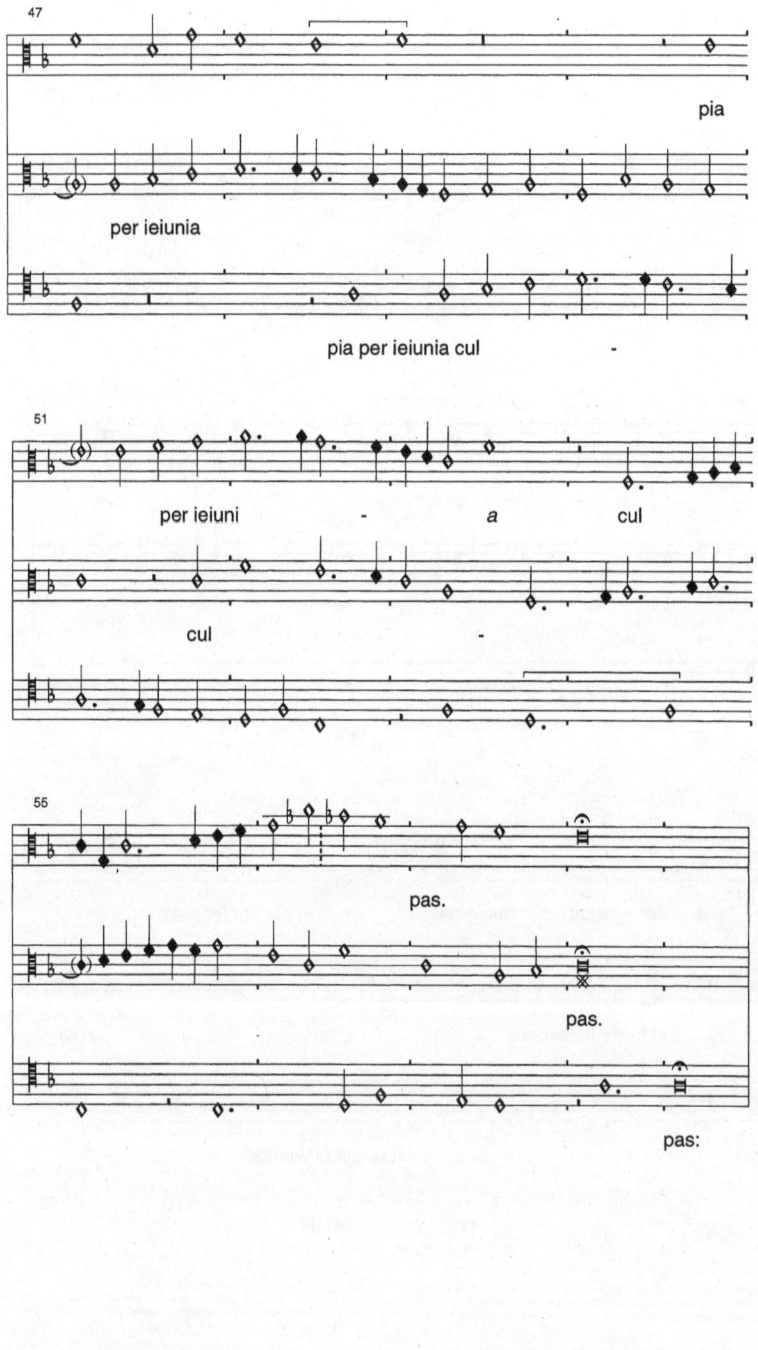
47
pia
per ieiunia
pia per ieiunia cul -
51
per ieiuni - a cul
cul -
55
pas.
pas.
pas:

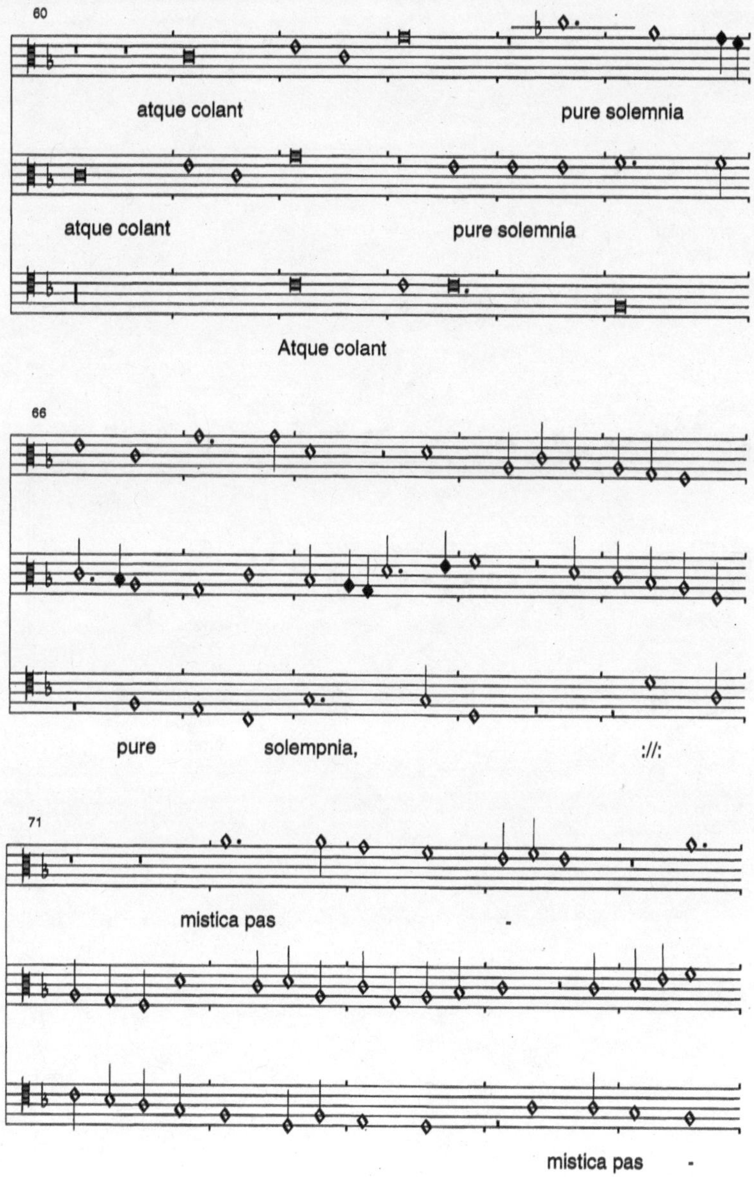
60
atque colant
pure solemnia
atque colant
pure solemnia
Atque colant
66
pure
solempnia,
://:
71
mistica pas
-
mistica pas
-

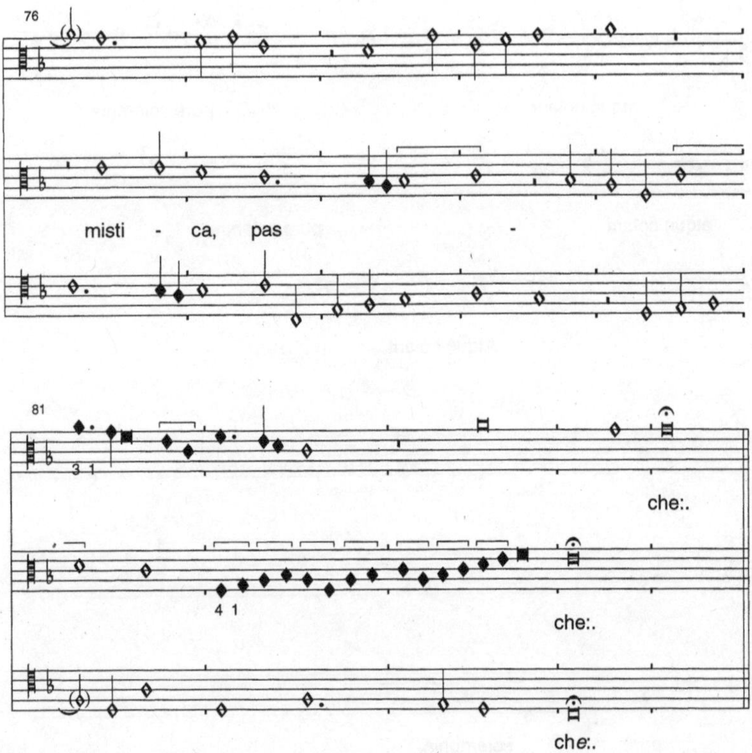
76
misti - ca, pas -
81
3 1
che:.
4 1
che:.
che:.

Plate 1: Cambridge, Trinity College, O.3.38, f. 12r

(reproduced by permission of the Master and Fellows of Trinity College, Cambridge)

Plate 2: Cambridge, Trinity College, O.3.38, f. 14r

(reproduced by permission of the Master and Fellows of Trinity College, Cambridge)

WORKS CITED

Books, Dissertations, and Editions

Aluas, Luminita Florea. "The *Quatuor principalia musicae*: A Critical Edition and Translation, with Introduction and Commentary." Ph.D. dissertation, Indiana University, 1996.

[Anonymous.] *The Pathway to Musicke*. London: William Barley, 1596.

[Anonymous.] *The solempnities. & triumphes doon & made at the spousellis and Mariage of the kyngis doughter the Ladye Marye to the Prynce of Castile Archeduke of Austrige*. London: Richarde Pynson, 1508; reprint in Roxburghe Club Publications, no. 23, London: Roxburghe Club, 1818.

Bathe, William. *A Briefe Introduction to the Skill of Song*. London: Thomas Este, (ca. 1587); reprint, with introduction by Bernarr Rainbow, Kilkenny: Boethius Press, 1982.

Bergsagel, John. *Early Tudor Masses: II*. Early English Church Music, vol. 16. London: Stainer and Bell, 1976.

Bernard, Edward. *Catalogi librorum manuscriptorum Anglie et Hibernie*. 2 vols. Oxford: Theatrum Sheldonianum, 1697.

Brewer, J. S. et al., eds. *Letters and Papers, Foreign and Domestic, of the Reign of Henry VIII*. 2d ed. London: H. M. Stationery Office, 1920.

Briquet, C. M. *Les Filigranes: Dictionnaire historique des marques du papier dès leur apparition vers 1282 jusqu'en 1600*. 4 vols. Paris Picard; Geneva: Jullien, 1907.

Busse Berger, Anna Maria. *Mensuration and Proportion Signs: Origins and Evolution*. Oxford: Clarendon Press; New York: Oxford University Press, 1993.

Carpenter, Nan Cooke. *Music in the Medieval and Renaissance Universities*. Norman: University of Oklahoma Press, 1958.

Coussemaker, Edmond de, ed. *Scriptorum de musica medii aevi nova series a Gerbertina altera*. 4 vols. Paris: Durand, 1864–76; reprint, Hildesheim: Olms, 1963.

Dumitrescu, Theodor. "Anglo-Continental Musical Relations, *c.* 1485–1530." 2 vols. D.Phil. thesis, University of Oxford, 2004.
To be published in a revised version as *The Early Tudor Court and International Musical Relations*. Aldershot: Ashgate, in press.

Emden, Alfred Brotherston. *A Biographical Register of the University of Oxford, A.D. 1501 to 1540*. Oxford: Clarendon Press, 1974.

Flood, W. H. Grattan. *Early Tudor Composers: Biographical Sketches of Thirty-Two Musicians and Composers of the Period 1485–1555*. London: Oxford University Press, 1925.

Frere, Walter Howard. *Antiphonale Sarisburiense*. London: Plainsong and Medieval Music Society, 1901–26.

Gaffurius, Franchinus. *De harmonia musicorum instrumentorum opus*. Milan: Gotardus Pontanus, 1518; reprint, New York: Broude Bros., 1979.

———. *Practica Musicae*. Trans. Clement A. Miller. Musicological Studies and Documents, no. 20. N.p.: American Institute of Musicology, 1968.

———. *Practica musice*. Milan: Ioannes Petrus de Lomatio, 1496; reprint, New York: Broude Bros., 1979.

———. *The "Practica musicae" of Franchinus Gafurius*. Translated by Irwin Young. Madison: University of Wisconsin Press, 1969.

Gasquet, Francis Aidan. *The Eve of the Reformation*. London: Bell, 1900; reprint, Port Washington, NY: Kennikat Press, 1971.

———. *Henry VIII and the English Monasteries*. Rev. ed. London: G. Bell, 1906.

Harrison, Frank Ll. *Music in Medieval Britain*. London: Routledge and Paul, 1958.

Hawkins, John. *A General History of the Science and Practice of Music*. 5 vols. London: T. Payne & Son, 1776; reprint, London: Novello, 1853.

Heawood, Edward. *Watermarks: Mainly of the 17th and 18th Centuries*. Monumenta chartæ papyraceæ historiam illustrantia, vol. 1. Hilversum: Paper Publications Society, 1950; reprint, 1981.

Helms, Dietrich. *Heinrich VIII. und die Musik*. Eisenach: Wagner, 1998.

Jackson, W. A.; F. S. Ferguson; and Katherine F. Pantzer, eds. *A Short-Title Catalogue of Books Printed in England, Scotland, & Ireland and of English Books Printed Abroad. 1475–1640*. 3 vols. 2d ed. London: The Bibliographical Society, 1976–91.

James, M. R. *The Ancient Libraries of Canterbury and Dover*. Cambridge: Cambridge University Press, 1903.

———. *The Western Manuscripts in the Library of Trinity College, Cambridge: A Descriptive Catalogue*. 4 vols. Cambridge: Cambridge University Press, 1900–1904.

London, British Library, R.M. 24.d.2. Facsimile edition with introduction by Jessie Ann Owens. Renaissance Music in Facsimile, vol. 8. New York: Garland, 1987.

Maynard, Judson. "An Anonymous Scottish Treatise on Music from the Sixteenth Century, British Museum Additional Manuscript 4911, Edition and Commentary." 2 vols. Ph.D. dissertation, Indiana University, 1961.

Meyer, Christian; Giuliano Di Bacco; Pia Ernstbrunner; Alexander Rauch; and Cesarino Ruini, eds. *The Theory of Music: Manuscripts from the Carolingian Era up to c.1500: Addenda, Corrigenda*. RISM BIII/6. Munich: Henle, 2003.

Meyer, Christian; Michel Huglo; and Nancy C. Phillips, eds. *The Theory of Music: Manuscripts from the Carolingian Era up to c.1500 in Great Britain and in the United States of America*. RISM BIII/4. Munich: Henle, 1992.

Morley, Thomas. *A Plain and Easy Introduction to Practical Music*. Edited by R. Alec Harman. 2d ed. London: J. M. Dent; New York: W. W. Norton, 1963.

Pace, Richard. *De fructu qui ex doctrina percipitur (The Benefit of a Liberal Education)*. Edited and translated by Frank Manley and Richard S. Sylvester. New York: Ungar, 1967.

Piccard, Gerhard. *Die Wasserzeichenkartei Piccard im Hauptstaatsarchiv Stuttgart*. Findbuch 17, *Wasserzeichen: Hand und Handschuh*. Stuttgart: W. Kohlhammer, 1997.

Reaney, Gilbert, ed. *Johannes Hothby, Opera omnia de musica mensurabili; Thomas Walsingham, Regulae de musica mensurabili*. Corpus scriptorum de musica, vol. 31. Neuhausen-Stuttgart: Hänssler Verlag for the American Institute of Musicology, 1983.

———, ed. *Johannes Hothby, Opera omnia de proportionibus; Anonymus, Tractatus de contrapunto (Ms. Venice, Lat. VIII.82, coll. 3047)*. Corpus scriptorum de musica, vol. 39. Neuhausen-Stuttgart: Hänssler Verlag for the American Institute of Musicology, 1997.

Reaney, Gilbert, and André Gilles, eds. *Tractatus de figuris sive de notis; Johannes Torkesey, Declaratio trianguli et scuti.* Corpus scriptorum de musica, vol. 12. N.p.: American Institute of Musicology, 1966.

Schillings, Arnold; E. H. J. Reusens; and Joseph Wils, eds. *Matricule de l'Université de Louvain.* 10 vols. in 18. Académie royale des sciences, des lettres et des beaux-arts de Belgique, Commission royale d'histoire, [Publications in-quarto], vol. 35. Brussels: Kiessling, 1903–80.

Stephen, Leslie, and Sidney Lee, eds., *Dictionary of National Biography ... from the Earliest Times to 1900.* 22 vols. London: Oxford University Press, 1949–50.

Tinctoris, Johannes. "Proportionale musices." In *Opera theoretica,* ed. Albert Seay, 2a:9–60. 3 vols. in 2. Corpus scriptorum de musica, vol. 22. N.p.: American Institute of Musicology, 1975–78.

Twyne, John. *De rebus Albionicis, Britannicis atque Anglicis, commentariorum libri duo.* London: Edm. Bollifantus, pro Richardo Watkins, 1590.

Urry, William. *Christopher Marlowe and Canterbury.* London: Faber, 1988.

Woodley, Ronald. *John Tucke: A Case Study in Early Tudor Music Theory.* Oxford: Clarendon Press; New York: Oxford University Press, 1993.

Articles

Bent, Margaret. "The Early Use of the Sign Φ." *Early Music* 24 (1996): 199–225.

———. "Notation, §III, 3: Polyphonic Mensural Notation, *c*1260–1500." In *The New Grove Dictionary of Music and Musicians,* 2d ed., ed. Stanley Sadie, 18:129–40. 29 vols. London: Macmillan, 2001.

———. "On the Interpretation of Φ in the Fifteenth Century." *Journal of the American Musicological Society* 53 (2000): 597–612.

Bray, Roger. "Editing and Performing *Musica Speculativa.*'" In *English Choral Practice, 1400–1650,* ed. John Morehen, 48–73. Cambridge: Cambridge University Press, 1995.

———. "Music and Musicians in Tudor England: Sources, Composition Theory and Performance." In *The Blackwell History of Music in Britain: The Sixteenth Century,* ed. Roger Bray, 1–45. Oxford: Blackwell, 1995.

———. "Music and the Quadrivium in Early Tudor England." *Music and Letters* 76 (1995): 1–18.

Charles, Sydney R. “The Provenance and Dates of the Pepys Ms. 1236.” *Musica disciplina* 16 (1962): 57–71.

Dart, Thurston. “Origines et sources de la musique de chambre en Angleterre (1500–1530).” In *La musique instrumentale de la Renaissance*, ed. Jean Jacquot, 77–84. Paris: Centre Nationale de la Recherche Scientifique, 1955.

Frampton, T. Shipdem. “St. Mary’s Church, Minster, Isle of Thanet: List of Vicars.” *Archaeologia Cantiana* 25 (1902): 97–112.

Hallmark, Rufus. “An Unknown English Treatise of the 16th Century.” *Journal of the American Musicological Society* 22 (1969): 273–74.

Hanna, Ralph. “Producing Magdalen College MS lat. 93.” *Yearbook of English Studies* 33 (2003): 142–55.

Harrison, Frank Ll. “Music at Oxford before 1500.” In *The History of the University of Oxford*, vol. 2, *Late Medieval Oxford*, ed. J. I. Catto and Ralph Evans, 347–71. Oxford: Clarendon Press, 1992; reprint, 1995.

———. “Music for the Sarum Rite: MS. 1236 in the Pepys Library, Magdalene College, Cambridge.” *Annales musicologiques* 6 (1958–63): 99–144.

Mathiesen, Thomas J. “‘The Office of the New Feast of Corpus Christi’ in the *Regimen Animarum* at Brigham Young University.” *Journal of Musicology* 2 (1983): 13–44.

Meech, Sanford B. “Three Musical Treatises in English from a Fifteenth-Century Manuscript.” *Speculum* 10 (1935): 265–69.

Questier, Michael. “Crypto-Catholicism, Anti-Calvinism and Conversion at the Jacobean Court: The Enigma of Benjamin Carier.” *Journal of Ecclesiastical History* 47 (1996): 45–64.

Sweeney, Cecily. “John Wylde and the Musica Guidonis,” *Musica disciplina* 29 (1977): 43–59.

Wathey, Andrew. “Notes on Discant and Mensuration from Fifteenth-Century Oxford.” In *Trent’anni di ricerca musicologica: Studi in onore di F. Alberto Gallo*, ed. Patrizia Dalla Vecchia and Donatella Restani, 63–72. Rome: Torre d’Orfeo, 1996.

Wegman, Rob C. “Different Strokes for Different Folks? On Tempo and Diminution in Fifteenth-Century Music.” *Journal of the American Musicological Society* 53 (2000): 461–505.

———. “What Is ‘acceleratio mensurae’?” *Music and Letters* 73 (1992): 515–24.

Woods, Isobel P. "A Note on 'Scottish Anonymous.'" *Royal Music Association Research Chronicle* 21 (1988): 37–39.

INDEX VERBORUM

INDEX NOMINUM ET RERUM

Studies in the History of Music Theory and Literature

Volume 1

Music and Ideas in the Sixteenth and Seventeenth Centuries
By Claude V. Palisca

Volume 2

John Dygon's *Proportiones practicabiles secundum Gaffurium*
Edited and translated by Theodor Dumitrescu